America's RISING STAR CHEFS

ROBERT MONDAVI PRESENTS

COOKING & ENTERTAINING WITH
America's
RISING STAR CHEFS

INTRODUCTION BY MARGRIT BIEVER
FOREWORD BY ROBERT MONDAVI

SANTA FE PUBLISHING
SAN FRANCISCO

ISBN 0-9641403-0-6: $19.95
Library of Congress Catalog Card Number: 94-67800

Manufactured in Canada
Distributed in Canada by Publishers Group West,
Emeryville, California

Photographer: William McKellar
Book Designer: Barbara Denney, *Southwest Passages Magazine*
Editor: Marsha Vande Berg
Stylists: Joseph Cunningham, Michael Rayner
Executive Chef: Gary Jenanyan
Sous Chef: Marvin D. Martin
Food Stylists: Gary Jenanyan, William McKellar
Indexer: Dennis Engel
Publishing Director: Brad Stauffer

Publisher: Anthony Tiano

CONTENTS

The recipes in this book follow the recipes in the
America's Rising Star Chefs television series. All recipes have
been tested by professional chefs.

*Napa Valley lends its own very special brand of joie de vivre to
food, wine and entertaining.*

ACKNOWLEDGMENTS

It takes hard work to do a television series or a book, and we
have done both in the summer of '94. We have delivered what
we hope will be a useful and informative video and print
experience that you will enjoy for years to come.

We salute the passion of these remarkable chefs.

The idea was shaped by Anthony Tiano,
Jim Lautz and Jon Holman of Santa Fe Ventures,
with help from Margrit Biever, Martin Johnson and
Axel Fabre of The Robert Mondavi Winery,
and John Porter, Bill Dale and Gene Nichols of
public television's innovative American Program Service.

We received support from
The Robert Mondavi Winery,
The American Program Service,
Farberware,
ITT Sheraton Corporation,
American Airlines and
G.E. Profile™ Appliances.

Products for the table settings were provided by:
Vanderbilt & Co. of The Napa Valley;
Baccarat, Inc.;
Villeroy & Boch Tableware Ltd.;
The Optima Company Ltd.;
and Necessities of New York.

Special thanks to my family, who pitched in
with support and cheer when it was most needed.
To Kat, Mark, Barbara, Steve and Kaleigh
Thanks.

Anthony Tiano

INTRODUCTION

by Margrit Biever

*Vice President of Cultural Affairs,
Robert Mondavi Winery*

What a joy it has been to watch this marvelous America's Rising Star Chefs concept become a reality through the efforts of so many talented and dedicated individuals. All of their efforts are reflected in this deliciously informative book and in the beautifully filmed public television series it documents — both of which honor the 13 recipients of our 1994 Robert Mondavi Culinary Award of Excellence.

Chefs truly are stars! They are cherished national treasures who transform a country's natural products into works of culinary art and who capture the spirit and energy — the heart and soul — of the people who live there. Artists and nurturers, the 13 Rising Star Chefs profiled here reflect the diversity of foods, culture and regional distinctiveness that make America so great. They all possess their own special genius and style in — and outside — the kitchen!

We all look to gurus, someone we can follow as an example and someone who provides not just instruction, but inspiration as well. These Rising Star Chefs *are* inspired and are leading the revolution in American cooking. I know you'll enjoy getting to know them better in the chapters that follow.

America's cooking scene is really so exciting with so many young chefs bringing fresh ideas and new interpretations of the classics to the table. As a member of this year's selection panel, I know what a difficult challenge it was limiting our choices to just 13 award winners. Fortunately, we'll have the opportunity to honor more young chefs next year and into the future.

Julia Child really started this whole renaissance in American cooking about 30 years ago. And beginning in the 1970s, California chefs Alice Waters and Jeremiah Tower, among others, taught us the importance of going to the garden and getting the best and the freshest ingredients possible. And in America, we are so lucky — we have everything — marvelous fish, fowl, beef, grains, fruits and vegetables.

As you are about to discover, this is a fun, informative and extremely functional guide to creating some very exciting foods. But it also is much more! It is a window to Napa Valley's unique lifestyle and its residents' panache for entertaining and sharing the good things in life.

It treats each meal — whether a casual country picnic, poolside Hawaiian lunch or elegant Mediterranean-inspired dinner party — as a celebration, offering theme and decor suggestions, along with spectacular menus and recipes. These details bring the food and the table together and treat your guests to a very special, pampered experience that is truly a feast for all of the senses!

Because wine makes a feast of any meal, each chapter includes suggestions on wine varietals to enjoy with the individual courses in the featured menus. Wine is one of life's simple pleasures and never should be intimidating — but it is true, too, that the more we learn about any subject, the greater our appreciation. Besides, learning is fun, so each chapter also offers tantalizing tips and information about wine.

Together, all the elements so eloquently presented here reflect the Robert Mondavi family's philosophy of wine and food. Robert Mondavi says, "Making good wine is a skill, a fine wine an art." We all believe wine is at its very best when enjoyed with the other arts — certainly the culinary arts, fine arts and of course, the fine art of conversation.

In style, the book and television series closely follow the essence of our 19-year-old Great Chefs program at the Robert Mondavi Winery. During these two- and three-day weekend events, a limited number of guests are treated to an elegant presentation of wine and food, featuring some of the world's most renowned chefs. It is a unique learning experience that encompasses all the essential elements of the good life, all enhanced by the natural beauty of Napa Valley.

While I am not a native of Napa Valley, it has been my adopted home for more than 30 years. Napa Valley is a truly special place that has captured my heart and brings fresh pleasures with each season — the blue-cast mountains of winter, the sunny yellow mustard of spring, the lush green vines of summer and the soft golden light of fall that follows another rich harvest.

It is with great pleasure that I invite you to discover a glimpse of Napa Valley in the pages that follow.

Enjoy in great health and joy!

FOREWORD
by Robert Mondavi

America's Rising Star Chefs is a source of great pride for me since it celebrates the Napa Valley and honors the up-and-coming great chefs of this country. It is my pleasure, on behalf of my family, to introduce them as the recipients of our first annual 1994 Robert Mondavi Culinary Award of Excellence.

My winegrowing career started in Napa Valley nearly 60 years ago at a time when wine critics, wine experts and consumers alike agreed that the only truly fine wines were grown in Europe. After 25 years in the wine business, I challenged that world view. I was convinced that Napa Valley possessed the climate, the soil, the grape varieties and the people to produce wines that belong in the company of the world's finest. Today, after years of dedicated research and experimentation by Napa Valley and California vintners, our wines are among the world's great wines, yet they possess their own distinct personality and style.

As the quality of American wines has evolved over the past 25 years, there has been increased international interest in our wines. But while we have made great progress, I say the best is yet to come! We will accomplish more in the next five years than we have in the past 15 years as we learn more and more about growing wines naturally in our vineyards. By implementing natural wine-growing methods, we are pro-

tecting the environment, the people who live and work in Napa Valley, and our future. These techniques are resulting in wines of enhanced quality — wines rich in varietal character with layers of complexity and flavor.

Today, our California wines, and specifically those of Napa Valley, are much more expressive of our great climate and soils than the "powerhouse" wines we produced in the 1970s. Today's wines are elegant and naturally balanced. They are gentle, harmonious and flavorful. They are accessible while young, yet they have great aging potential.

These are wines that truly enhance, not overpower, the wonderful and diverse foods our talented American chefs are creating.

The appreciation of wine and food — the awareness of the integral role the table plays in the quality of our daily lives, our happiness — is relatively new in America. Beginning in 1966, the year we built our winery in Oakville, and continuing through the 1980s, this country experienced a wine and food revolution. The packaged and over-processed TV dinners of the 1950s were replaced with a demand for seasonally fresh foods, regional specialties and the very best wines to go with them.

In fact, it was our new California cuisine, the inspiration of San Francisco Bay Area chefs Alice Waters, Jeremiah Tower and a handful of others, that really started it all. Suddenly chefs and vintners alike took on celebrity status! While the excitement of the 1970s and 1980s has calmed down a bit, America's tables have changed forever. Most importantly, as a nation, we are learning that the table provides one of life's great pleasures.

Dining allows us to savor each other's company, to refine the art of conversation, to slow down and get in touch with life's sensory aspects. Wine has become and will continue to be an essential part of gracious dining — whether it's a simple mid-week family meal at home or a more formal dinner celebration.

Fueling this increased interest in wine are recently published medical studies which confirm that for most people, wine enjoyed in moderation is not only good, but good for us. Wine not only enhances food, but medical studies now show that in moderation it helps digestion, protects the heart and reduces stress.

We also believe wine encourages camaraderie and sparks romance. After all, wine is a natural agricultural product which has been part of civilization for more than 7,000 years and which will continue to be integral to civilized life. Through the centuries, wine has been praised by poets, philosophers, scholars and statesmen.

Wine is the mealtime beverage of moderation to be enjoyed at the family table, as well as at more elaborate celebrations. It is part of religious ceremonies. It is chosen by leaders of one government when toasting another. Wine is the natural beverage for toasting those special moments, both grand and small — birthdays, graduations, engagements, weddings, anniversaries, promotions and family gatherings.

Wine is the only beverage that feeds our body and stimulates our spirit. It adds creativity, pleasure and happiness to our way of life. In enjoying wine, we participate in one of life's simple pleasures — a pleasure that will last a lifetime. What better way to celebrate than to pop a cork?

I truly believe America, with its innovative and diverse wines and food, can and will become the shining light for a new generation of consumers worldwide. We are blessed with bountiful natural resources and with a marvelous blend of ethnic and regional influences to flavor our pot!

We're equally blessed with the people — these 13 Rising Star Chefs — who are creating so much excitement with their new American cooking. I salute each of them for their innovative spirit and inspired dishes.

Besides capturing the essence of these talented chefs, this book reflects the casual elegance of Napa Valley's lifestyle and illustrates the simple pleasures a bottle of wine brings to the table, along with good food, good friends and family. In short, it encompasses all those things that make life — the good life — worth living.

To your health and happiness!

ROMANTIC
WINE COUNTRY PICNIC
FOR TWO

Featuring Nancy Oakes, Boulevard
San Francisco, California

Grilled Quail on Olive Branches with Roasted Peppers and Artichoke Salad

"I come from a family that really loves to cook."
—*Nancy Oakes*

Nancy Oakes recognizes that today's restaurant patrons want more than innovative food when they dine out. They also require a sophisticated dining experience. Oakes' Boulevard, a French bistro in downtown San Francisco, surrounds this chef's unique culinary style with savoir faire. Designed with business partner Pat Kuleto, Boulevard is located in the city's Audiffred Building, an 1889 French Mansard-style structure with a quirky place in local lore. It was spared from ruin in the fire and earthquake of 1906 after firefighters were bribed with a barrel of liquor. Its upstairs was headquarters for Harry Bridges and his International Long-

~ M E N U ~

*Seafood Sausage Arugula Salad
with Truffle Vinaigrette*

Robert Mondavi Carneros Chardonnay

*Grilled Quail on Olive Branches
with Roasted Peppers
and Artichoke Salad*

*Goat Cheese Grilled in Grape Leaves
with Wild Mushrooms
and Crispy Roast-Garlic Ravioli*

Robert Mondavi Carneros Pinot Noir

*Plum Brioche Bread Pudding
with Blackberries and Crème Fraîche*

Robert Mondavi Moscato d'Oro

family moved from the East Coast to California in 1969 when Oakes was 11 years old. She remembers that in times of "dire disaster," her mother would smooth over difficulties with distractions. "Now, what was that buttermilk pudding recipe?" she would ask.

Oakes, a Boston native, is a self-taught chef who did not think about cooking professionally until after she had worked a number of jobs to support herself. By the time she was cooking for Northern California longshoremen and roadies who worked for promoter Bill Graham in San Francisco, she clearly was headed toward a culinary career. That was 1978, and a "kinder and gentler time," before the food craze created whirls around celebrity chefs and restaurants as entertainment, says Oakes. It also was a time when women across the country were beginning to establish independent careers as chefs and restaurant owners.

That same year, Oakes took over the kitchen in a lively neighborhood bar, Pat O'Shea's Mad Hatter. Later, she jumped next door to open the French-inspired L'Avenue. She has since closed L'Avenue, taking her staff with her to the downtown Boulevard.

Through her various evolutions, there has been a consistency to the magic Oakes performs in the kitchen. She says it derives from an intuitive sense about how to balance flavors. It also comes from knowing that food that is designed does not always appeal to a diner's sense of taste. "One of the dangers in being a chef during these times is in thinking that there's always something new around the corner. There probably isn't.

"There's probably good reason why the classic dishes still will be around long after salmon tartare with jicama sauce has come and gone," says Oakes.

shoreman's Association during the deadly 1934 strike. Boulevard is industrial art nouveau in design. It was built as if it were in the Eiffel Tower, says Kuleto, San Francisco's celebrity restaurant designer.

Inside Boulevard, dark woods and a glass-bedecked bar harmonize with Oakes' bistro menus. Served in generous portions, her food is blessed by freshness and innovation. Truffle vinaigrette or seafood sausage made with morels can be featured items alongside food reminiscent of the tastes from America's heartland. "There's a lot of good, old American food that's forgotten about, and yet it's truly wonderful," says Oakes.

Oakes' cooking style and the restaurant she works in demonstrate an understanding for what she says Americans want. More and more, people are preferring food that reminds them of home to overly designed food. The key is to make food available in an environment that is appealing, comfortable and coated with a cosmopolitan veneer.

In Oakes' family, food was synonymous with love. Her

SEAFOOD SAUSAGE ARUGULA SALAD
WITH TRUFFLE VINAIGRETTE

SAUSAGE

| 12 | oz. fresh salmon, boned and skinned |
| 1 | egg white, well chilled |

*Let the picnic and the romance begin with
Nancy Oakes' menu and Robert Mondavi wine.*

¾ cup whipping cream, well chilled
½ tsp. ground black pepper
2 tsp. kosher salt
¼ cup cooked lobster meat, cut into ¼" dice
½ cup sea scallops, cut into ¼" pieces
½ cup fresh morels, roasted (recipe follows)
1 Tbs. Pernod or other anise-flavored liqueur
¼ tsp. fennel seed, ground
1½ Tbs. chives, minced
1 Tbs. fresh tarragon, chopped

¼ cup fresh parsley, finely chopped
1 36" piece sausage casing

Chill food processor bowl and metal blade for 30 minutes. Cut 8 ounces of salmon into ½-inch cubes and the remaining 4 ounces into ¼-inch cubes. Freeze the large pieces for 15 minutes. Keep remaining salmon in refrigerator. In the chilled bowl, process the partially frozen large chunks of salmon until smooth. With motor running, add egg white and slowly pour in cream until incorporated.

Add salt and pepper. Stop machine and transfer mixture

Napa Valley: The Evolution of a Great Winegrowing Region

"We in the United States can make as great a variety of wines as are made in Europe—not exactly the same kinds, but doubtless as good." Those are the words of Thomas Jefferson, America's far-sighted, wine-loving third president.

Some 200 years later, his words are prophetic. Wines from California's Napa Valley, America's premier winegrowing region, now rank among the world's great wines. Compared to wine's 7,000-year history, California's wine industry is in its infancy. In 1994, Napa Valley, which is only 30 miles long and five miles wide, celebrates just 156 years of winegrowing.

While small in geographical size, it is a giant when measured by the extraordinary natural resources it has for growing outstanding wines. Those resources include an ideal climate with microclimates suitable for the cultivation of a

Robert Mondavi

number of grape varieties, well-drained soils and people with a passion to excel, according to Napa Valley's legendary vintner Robert Mondavi.

It was Northern California's Gold Rush in 1848 that initially brought European immigrants to the region. They, in turn, paved the way for the cultivation of the vineyards'

liquid gold. The now-legendary winemakers Charles Krug, Otto Beringer and Jacob Schram are among the Germans who brought Old World winegrowing traditions to Napa Valley.

While these early pioneers used simple techniques, their wines earned international recognition. Napa Valley wines garnered 20 of the 34 medals awarded to California wines at the Exposition Universelle in Paris in 1889. One year later, nearly half the California wines entered in the Paris Exposition won gold medals.

However, two major setbacks followed: Phylloxera and Prohibition. Phylloxera, a pest that destroys the roots of vines, was found in Napa Valley vineyards in the late 1800s. By the early 1900s, it had ravaged the vineyards and required the costly and timely replanting of a Phylloxera-resistant root stock.

Meanwhile, Prohibition put an abrupt halt to the wine industry's progress. Pre-Prohibition Napa Valley boasted 120 wineries, but by 1933, when Prohibition was repealed, there were only 48. The survivors faced difficult years of re-discovering the traditions that form the art of winegrowing.

By the mid-1960s, Napa Valley vintners rocked the wine world again with distinctive fine wines. Napa Valley varietals were back — taking top awards at prestigious international tastings.

Today, there are 200 wineries in Napa Valley and some 700 throughout California. While Napa Valley again has earned its place as one of the world's great wine regions, most vintners predict the best is yet to come as research and experimentation lend greater focus to growing wines naturally.

to a bowl. Fold in lobster, scallops and roasted morel mushrooms and remaining salmon. Fold in Pernod, fennel, chives, tarragon and parsley. To test mixture, make a small patty and poach in simmering water for 4 minutes. Adjust seasoning to taste.

With a pastry bag and large open tip, pipe mixture into casings. Tie into 4- to 5-inch links or roll in plastic wrap to form 4- to 5-inch links. Twist and knot the ends. Poach sausage in simmering water, weighed down with kitchen towel, for 10 minutes. Reserve.

ROASTED MORELS

½ lb. morels or other wild mushrooms
1 tsp. garlic, chopped
2 Tbs. olive oil
1 Tbs. fresh thyme, chopped
2 Tbs. water
salt and pepper

Toss all ingredients together, place on baking sheet and bake in pre-heated 425-degree oven 7 minutes. Remove from oven and reserve.

TRUFFLE VINAIGRETTE

4 Tbs. olive oil
1 shallot, finely diced
1 small clove garlic, pressed
½ oz. black truffle, grated
2 Tbs. sherry vinegar
1 Tbs. parsley, finely chopped
salt and pepper

In a sauté pan, heat 1 tablespoon olive oil. Add shallot, garlic and truffle. Sauté. Cool. Add vinegar, whisk in remaining olive oil, add parsley and season with salt and pepper. Reserve.

FOR THE SALAD

2 handfuls arugula
¼ head radicchio
1 cup frisee

To Serve: Brush sausage with oil and grill or sauté until golden. Season vinaigrette with salt and pepper, then dress the salad. Place sausage on plate and garnish with salad. Serve.

(Seafood Sausage recipe adapted from "Hot Links and

Seafood Sausage, Arugula Salad with Truffle Vinaigrette

Country Flavors," written by Bruce Aidells and Denis Kelly, published by Knopf, New York, 1990.)

GRILLED QUAIL ON OLIVE BRANCHES WITH ROASTED PEPPERS AND ARTICHOKE SALAD

QUAIL

2 large boneless quail
1 large red pepper

Combine marinade ingredients (recipe follows). Add quail and marinate at least 2 hours or overnight. Skewer quail on olive branches, rosemary branches or skewers soaked in water. Brush quail with marinade and grill each side approximately 6 minutes over a medium fire. Remove from fire and place on plate. Pour sherry sauce (recipe follows) over quail. Brush again and return quail to the grill for one minute more on each side. Warm the marinated peppers (recipe follows) on the grill. Save all liquids that collect on the plate. Reserve.

MARINADE FOR QUAIL

4 cloves garlic, crushed
2 sprigs rosemary
2 Tbs. olive oil
1 Tbs. coarsely ground pepper

SHERRY SAUCE

1	cup dry sherry
¼	cup sherry vinegar
3	shallots, coarsely chopped
2	sprigs fresh thyme
6	black peppercorns
3	whole cloves garlic, peeled and crushed

Combine ingredients in heavy saucepan. Reduce over medium heat to ½ cup. Strain through fine strainer, pressing the solids from the liquid. Cool and reserve.

MARINADE FOR RED PEPPER

1	clove garlic, thinly sliced
1	Tbs. fresh thyme leaves
3	large basil leaves
2	Tbs. extra virgin olive oil
	salt and freshly ground pepper

Blacken the skin of the pepper over the open flame of a gas burner or under the broiler. This should be done with very high heat and very quickly so that the meat of the pepper does not get overcooked. Place in paper bag for 10 minutes. Peel away the burned skin. Cut the pepper in half and clean thoroughly.

Combine marinade ingredients in a small glass bowl. Add grilled pepper and marinate at least 2 hours. Remove from marinade and slice into strips. Reserve.

ARTICHOKE SALAD

10	young artichokes, small enough so choke has not developed
1	lemon, zested and juiced
¼	cup light olive oil
1	cup yellow onion, finely diced
1	cup hot water
¼	cup English peas, shelled
¼	cup fava beans, shelled
3	small mint leaves, cut into chiffonade
2	Tbs. extra-virgin olive oil
5	cups water
	salt and pepper

Trim artichokes and remove rough outer leaves. Slice artichokes ⅛-inch thick and put into acidulated water, made with 4 cups of water and ½ of the lemon juice. Reserve.

Heat light olive oil in a heavy saucepan. Add onions and sauté until soft, but not brown. Add drained artichokes. Sauté 3 minutes, moistening with 1 cup hot water. Bring mixture to a boil, cover and cook for five minutes, then uncover and cook until water is almost evaporated.

Add peas and fava beans and season with salt and pepper. Toss vegetables, cover and cook for 2 minutes until tender. Spread on a baking pan to cool. When mixture is at room temperature, transfer to a bowl. Add 1 tablespoon lemon juice, 1 tablespoon julienned lemon zest, mint leaves and 2 tablespoons extra-virgin olive oil. Taste for seasoning. Add more lemon juice if needed. Reserve.

To Serve: Spoon one serving of the artichoke salad onto each plate. Place a quail on the salad and drizzle the sherry sauce and reserved juices (from the grilled quail plate) over the salad. Garnish the plate with the roasted pepper slices and serve.

GOAT CHEESE GRILLED IN GRAPE LEAVES WITH WILD MUSHROOMS AND CRISPY ROAST-GARLIC RAVIOLI

GOAT CHEESE GRILLED IN GRAPE LEAVES

4	6″ grape leaves, blanched
3	oz. goat cheese
4	dry-cured olives, pitted and sliced
2	Tbs. sun-dried tomatoes in olive oil, julienned
2	Tbs. olive oil
	freshly ground black pepper

Lay two grape leaves side by side, overlapping. Place 1½ ounces of goat cheese in the center and sprinkle with ½ of the olives and tomatoes. Fold leaves around cheese. Brush with olive oil and secure by wrapping in plastic wrap. Repeat and reserve until ready to grill.

RAVIOLI

2	Tbs. olive oil
1	large head of garlic
8	wonton skins of thin, fresh pasta (available in specialty stores)
1	egg white, lightly beaten

Details Can Make The Difference

A picnic for two is romantic by definition, and to enjoy this outing simply keep in mind that the small touches make the impact. Here is a list of items to enhance your romantic picnic:

- floral foam (oasis) and ribbon
- plastic bucket and picnic basket
- 20 stems garden roses
- 10 stems Queen Anne's lace
- 10 stems blue lace
- 30 stems lavender and 1 bunch statice
- 1 large tablecloth and tarpaulin
- 2 basket trays
- 2 place mats, 2 napkins
- throw pillows

1. If you have a divided picnic basket, use one side to hold a jar of wildflowers, which you picked in the countryside or bought while grocery shopping.

By all means, arrange the flowers at the picnic site, using the oasis and a jar that were packed in with the food. Use a snippet of ribbon as a napkin ring and also to tie a flower to each napkin.

2. Cloth napkins always are preferred, and colorful acrylic plates can add a touch of fun and fancy. Bring a throw pillow or two for that lazy afternoon nap.

3. Protect your tablecloth by spreading a tarpaulin on the ground first. And in the likely event that your picnic site is not entirely on level ground, a tray or two will be a welcome addition to your picnic.

3   cups vegetable oil for frying
salt and pepper

Pre-heat oven to 350 degrees. Brush garlic with olive oil and season with salt and pepper. Wrap in foil and roast 1 hour. Cut off root end of the bulb and squeeze roasted garlic from the skin. Mash the garlic with a fork and season with salt and pepper.

Using a brush or finger, outline one wonton skin with egg white. Place $1/2$ teaspoon of garlic in the center and fold the wonton skin into a triangle. Press firmly to seal edges. Repeat with remaining wonton skins and garlic. (Uncooked ravioli may be made up to two days in advance and refrigerated, uncovered, on a baking sheet dusted with cornstarch or rice flour.)

In a heavy pan, heat 1 inch of oil to 375 degrees. Fry ravioli until golden, turning once. Drain well and sprinkle with salt. (Do not refrigerate or wrap in plastic. Ravioli must be cooked and eaten on the same day.)

ROASTED MUSHROOMS

$1^1/2$ cups wild mushrooms (chanterelle, porcini, shiitake or portabello)
1   Tbs. garlic, finely chopped
1   Tbs. fresh thyme leaves
2   Tbs. olive oil
2   Tbs. water
salt and pepper

Pre-heat oven to 425 degrees. Clean mushrooms. Trim and slice. Toss in a bowl with garlic, thyme, olive oil, water, salt and pepper. Spread mixture on a baking pan and roast for 7 minutes. Cool and reserve at room temperature.

To Serve: Remove plastic from goat cheese wrapped in grape leaves and season with salt and pepper. Grill 3 minutes on each side over medium fire, or broil.

Divide mushrooms between two plates. Open up leaves around the goat cheese and serve next to mushrooms. Eat, using ravioli as a scoop.

PLUM BRIOCHE BREAD PUDDING
WITH BLACKBERRIES AND CRÈME FRAÎCHE

PUDDING

2   2" thick slices of brioche or egg bread, cut to

match the diameter of ramekins
1   dark red firm plum, halved, pitted and cut into 10 slices
2   8 oz. ramekins

CUSTARD

3   eggs, beaten
1   cup milk
$1/2$ cup cream
$1/4$ tsp. vanilla extract
2   Tbs. sugar

In a shallow bowl, whisk together eggs, milk, cream, vanilla extract and sugar. Place brioche or egg bread rounds into mixture. Turn bread over in mixture until it is soaked and most of the liquid is absorbed. Reserve.

CARAMEL

$1/2$ cup sugar
$1/4$ cup unsalted butter
1   vanilla bean, split and scraped
1   dark red firm plum, chopped

In a heavy saucepan, melt butter with sugar over medium heat. Add vanilla bean and cook until mixture is bubbling. Add chopped plum and continue cooking for two more minutes. Lower heat and cook mixture for 5 more minutes. Remove from heat and strain caramel through a fine strainer. Scrape any remaining seeds from the bean pod into the caramel. Reserve.

Pre-heat oven to 375 degrees. Arrange reserved plum slices in the bottom of two ramekins. Add enough caramel to cover. Gently place custard-soaked brioche on top. Bake in oven center until golden and puffed, approximately 45 minutes.

GARNISH

1   cup blackberries
$1/4$ cup crème fraîche or sour cream

To Serve: Puddings are best when served warm. On a picnic, set ramekins off to the side of the grill to warm. Invert each onto a serving plate and garnish with berries and crème fraîche. Serve.

ELEGANT SEAFOOD DINNER FOR SIX

Featuring George Morrone, Aqua
San Francisco, California

Aqua Crabcakes

For George Morrone, consistency is a key ingredient to success — as restaurateur, chef and fisherman. The chef and part-owner of Aqua, in San Francisco, practices the steady art of applying himself fully to the task at hand—be that pairing tuna with a Pinot Noir sauce or trolling the ocean's depths for tarpon and bone fish.

As the availability of choices has increased at a pace equal to exposure to various ethnic cuisines, chefs like Morrone have reeled from the impact on Americans' expectations when it comes to food. As a result, many emphasize uniqueness and boldness in both taste and presentation.

~ MENU ~

Aqua Crabcakes

Robert Mondavi Napa Valley Fumé Blanc

Oven-Roasted Oysters,
Sweet Onion Puree, Beurre Rouge

Robert Mondavi Carneros Pinot Noir

Ahi Tuna Niçoise Salad
with Black Olive Tapenade

Robert Mondavi Napa Valley Merlot

Crème Brulée

Robert Mondavi Napa Valley
Sauvignon Blanc Botrytis

ness, or ahi tuna that has just been caught off the Hawaiian coast. Its flavor is straightforward, pure and certainly fresh, he says.

Morrone's choice, whether for his own dinner or for his guests, is elegance wrapped in simplicity. His beguiling secret is in the execution—whether that be a classic crème brulée or an entree of oven-roasted oysters and caramelized onions served with beurre rouge. The basis for a successful crème brulée is not to rush it. With the oyster and onion dish, Morrone strives to balance acidity in the sauce with the onions' natural sweetness, which is brought out during the long cooking process.

Morrone's beginnings as a chef were hardly auspicious. It all started in the family business, a neighborhood dry cleaners in Maywood, New Jersey. Morrone worked there as a youth and hated it so much, "I got myself fired every week." The tension with his father drove him next door to John the baker. There he got a job, training in how to make Danish, bake bread and decorate cakes, and some advice. "Don't end up working every day, 11 p.m. to 7 a.m.," the baker told him.

Morrone took the advice, and after completing the 600 hours of routine restaurant work required as part of his application, he signed up at the Culinary Institute of America, in Hyde Park, New York. There he learned the classics and the basics. When he graduated, he anticipated it would take him a lifetime to reach the pinnacle enjoyed by his teachers.

As it turned out, Morrone spent the next decade patiently climbing the culinary ladder. "I was a cook for a long, long time. Then I was a sous chef, then a chef and now I'm a restaurateur."

From Brooklyn Heights' River Café, with a view of Manhattan's skyline from across the East River, Morrone arrived in San Francisco to work with culinary star Bradley Ogden, then the chef at Campton Place. That was 1986. An opportunity to be executive chef at the swanky Los Angeles Hotel Bel-Air beckoned before long, however.

At Bel-Air, Morrone played culinary host to the stars, the tourists, and the movers and shakers intent on power dining. Two years later, he returned to San Francisco, with part ownership of Aqua in his pocket. It was 1991, and the world was unfolding at his feet.

Today, Morrone believes, as he did while a student at the Culinary Institute, that chefs are made, not born. Ability and creativity evolve in the kitchen. Whether it is cooking or

But those who succeed are those who offer a certain consistency when it comes to quality. "Today, cooking is more thought-out. Cooks and chefs are a little more sincere. They are not experimenting blindly," says Morrone.

It was a bold decision to open Aqua in the heart of San Francisco's Financial District, already replete with tantalizing restaurant choices. Likewise, it was bold to offer only a seafood menu, while turning certain culinary traditions upside down.

Only one fish on the menu is grilled. Red wines are matched with fish. Fish is treated like meat and served with sauces that are based on veal and chicken stock. Foie gras—paired with fish—may be served more at Aqua than at any other restaurant in the United States. "I wanted to change people's expectations of what going to a fish restaurant is all about," says Morrone.

His personal favorite? It certainly is not crabcakes. "I hate them," he says. This chef, whose combinations bring sophistication to a new level, prefers oysters, with their characteristic brini-

Ahi Tuna Niçoise Salad and Black Olive Tapenade is served with Robert Mondavi Carneros Pinot Noir.

Morrone's avocational passion —fishing— the critical element is consistency.

"There's nothing that has not been done before. It's really a matter of how it all gets put together," says Morrone.

AQUA CRABCAKES

MAYONNAISE

2	egg yolks
1	whole egg
2	tsp. Dijon mustard

$\frac{1}{8}$	tsp. cayenne pepper
2	Tbs. lemon juice
12	oz. olive oil

In a food processor, blend egg yolk, egg, mustard, cayenne and lemon juice until smooth. With machine running, add oil in a small, steady stream, processing until mixture is completely emulsified. Transfer to a bowl, season with salt and refrigerate.

BASIL MAYONNAISE

$\frac{1}{2}$	cup mayonnaise (recipe above)
$1\frac{1}{2}$	Tbs. basil oil (see Ahi Tuna Salad recipe)

White Wine Follows Its Own Odyssey

All great wines are grown in the vineyard and are born of outstanding fruit. In growing the best white wines, winemakers typically pursue an expression of crisp, bright varietal flavors.

White winemaking differs from red wine production in that it requires less time but greater precaution against oxidation. Unprotected by tannin or its own strong character, white wine must be handled from the start with great care and under cool, clean conditions.

Even in the vineyard, coolness is white wine's greatest friend. Indeed, the typically cooler regions of California, France, Germany and Italy have produced the best white wines of the world.

At harvest, white grapes are picked during the cool, early morning hours and early in the season. Brought to the winery, the grapes are crushed gently, removing the cluster from its bitter stalk. Unless a full-bodied white wine is being cultivated, the skins and seeds are removed from the must within a few hours, and the wine is immediately pressed. The "free-run," or juice that naturally collects before the pressing, is of the highest quality.

Again, coolness is vital, this time in the fermentation process. Unlike the more stable red wine, white wine is more dependent on fragile and volatile components. By lowering the temperature in the fermenting tanks to 55 degrees, winemakers retain the fresh varietal fruit flavors and natural acid/sugar balance while keeping any bitter, undesirable by-products from developing.

White wine fermentation lasts from three to five days, unlike the process for red wines, which takes a week and sometimes longer. When fermentation is completed, the wine is racked or transferred to another tank or barrel to achieve clarity. The "lees," or yeast remnants, are left in the bottom of the tank.

For added complexity and depth, white wine varietals such as Chardonnay, Fumé Blanc and Sauvignon Blanc are fermented in the barrel. Some wineries age these wines on their lees for additional richness. Prior to bottling, white wines often are filtered.

However, with gentle care and exceptional quality fruit, a fine wine may be bottled unfiltered, allowing winemakers to retain the wine's natural body, texture, aromas and flavors.

After fermentation, cool, dry conditions and good timing are equally important. Delicate, fruity white wines reach perfection quickly and begin to lose their desirable fresh, young character in two to five years. Some bottle aging is desirable, especially for more firmly structured white wines.

White wines generally are extremely versatile and may be enjoyed with a variety of foods. Balance is the key.

In a stainless steel or glass bowl, whisk together mayonnaise and basil oil. Reserve.

CRABCAKE MIX

2	Tbs. olive oil
1	stalk celery, finely diced
1/2	medium onion, finely diced
1	lb. lump crabmeat
1/2	cup mayonnaise (recipe above)
2	Tbs. Italian parsley, chopped
1	Tbs. chives, minced finely
1	cup panko (large white) bread crumbs
	salt and pepper

Heat olive oil in a sauté pan, add celery and onion and sauté until just soft. Remove from heat.

In a large bowl, thoroughly mix crabmeat, 1/2 cup mayonnaise, parsley, chives and bread crumbs with celery and onion mixture. Season with salt and pepper. Form into cakes approximately 1 1/2 inches high and 2 inches wide. Reserve.

BREADING

4	eggs, beaten
4	cups panko bread crumbs
6	Tbs. Wondra flour
	salt and pepper
	oil for frying

Place beaten eggs into a wide-mouthed bowl. Put bread crumbs and flour in separate pie plates or other containers.

Roll formed cakes first in flour, then in beaten eggs, then in bread crumbs, each time shaking off excess. Place on dry surface and chill until ready to fry.

TOMATO SALAD

8	Roma tomatoes peeled, seeded and diced
3	shallots, finely diced
1	Tbs. garlic, minced
3	Tbs. olive oil
6	basil leaves, cut into chiffonade
3	Tbs. balsamic vinegar
	salt and pepper

Heat olive oil in a small saucepan. Add tomatoes, shallots

Tuna Niçoise Salad with Tapenade

and garlic. Cook over very low heat until tomatoes are just cooked through. Remove from heat and cool.

In a stainless steel bowl, combine basil chiffonade and balsamic vinegar with tomato mixture. Season with salt and pepper and reserve.

To Serve: In a deep saucepan, heat oil for frying to 350 degrees. Fry crabcakes, four at a time, until golden brown. Drain on paper towels.

With a teaspoon, dot four corners of the inner rim of each plate with basil mayonnaise. Place 2 tablespoons of tomato salad in center of each plate. Place 2 crabcakes on top of tomato salad and drizzle basil oil (from Ahi Tuna Salad recipe) around cakes. Serve immediately.

OVEN-ROASTED OYSTERS, SWEET ONION PUREE, BEURRE ROUGE

OYSTERS

24	oysters, shucked and held in oyster liquor (Reserve bottom shells)

ONION PUREE

1½	Tbs.	butter
1½		large yellow onions, peeled, cut into ½" thin slices
3	Tbs.	red wine vinegar
1	Tbs.	fresh tarragon, chopped

Melt butter in a heavy sauté pan over low heat. Add onions and cook until caramelized, scraping the pan often to prevent burning.

Deglaze pan with red wine vinegar. Stir in tarragon. Remove from heat and puree mixture in food processor. Pass through a fine strainer. Season with salt and pepper and reserve.

BEURRE ROUGE

2	cups Robert Mondavi Pinot Noir
½	cup red wine vinegar
½	cup mushroom stems
6	shallots, sliced
6	white peppercorns, cracked
6	coriander seeds, cracked
2	thyme sprigs
1	bay leaf
4	Tbs. whipping cream
½	lb. unsalted butter, chilled, cut into cubes

In a non-reactive saucepan, combine wine, vinegar, mushroom stems, shallots, peppercorns, coriander, thyme and bay leaf. Over medium heat, reduce by ¾. Add whipping cream and reduce this quantity by ½. Lower heat and whisk in chilled butter, two cubes at a time, stirring constantly until sauce is emulsified. Strain and reserve.

GARNISH

3	cups rock salt
½	cup assorted spices: star anise, whole cloves, bay, whole fennel seeds

To Serve: Pre-heat oven to 450 degrees. Toss rock salt and spices together in a bowl and transfer mixture to a baking sheet. Place ½ teaspoon of onion puree in bottom of each oyster shell. Place an oyster in each shell.

Put oysters with shells on top of rock salt mixture and bake at 450 degrees until oysters are warmed through. Remove from oven. Divide salt mixture among six individual serving bowls. Arrange 4 oysters in each bowl and nap each with beurre rouge. Serve immediately.

AHI TUNA NIÇOISE SALAD WITH BLACK OLIVE TAPENADE

AHI TUNA

2	lbs. ahi tuna, cut into 12 medallions
4	oz. arugula

TAPENADE

½	cup Niçoise olives, pitted
3	cloves garlic, roasted
1	Tbs. fresh oregano, chopped
1	tsp. lemon juice
2	Tbs. extra-virgin olive oil
	salt and pepper

Place olives, roasted garlic, oregano and lemon juice in food processor. Add olive oil and blend to a fine consistency. Do not puree. Season with salt and pepper and reserve.

NIÇOISE VEGETABLES

10	green beans, finely diced, then blanched
3	medium zucchini, finely diced
1	large red bell pepper, roasted, peeled and diced
1	large yellow bell pepper, roasted, peeled and diced
8	halves small sun-dried tomatoes, diced

BALSAMIC VINAIGRETTE

1	Tbs. shallots
2	Tbs. balsamic vinegar
1	tsp. lemon juice
2	Tbs. Dijon mustard
1	scant cup olive oil
	salt and pepper

Sweat shallots briefly in a sauté pan in a small amount of olive oil. In a stainless steel or glass bowl, combine balsamic vinegar, lemon juice, mustard and shallots. Whisk in 1 scant cup of olive oil in a slow, steady stream to emulsify. Season with salt and pepper and reserve.

Shells and Sand Extend Party Theme

When elegance describes the dinner, a centerpiece augments the pleasure guests take
in the food, the wine and the company seated around the table. In this instance, the table setting
and an extension of the decor on the mantelpiece can set the stage for a delightful evening.
Here are the materials, followed by directions for making sand candles:

- sand and a shallow dish
- $\frac{1}{2}$" brick floral foam (oasis)
- 1 3"x5" beeswax candle
- 3 sand candles
- 3 bleached manzanita branches
- assorted seashells and coral

The focus is on light colors and linking the decor to the seafood dinner. Since the dinner is formal, place cards can be an important addition, particularly if guests do not know each other well. Here, a seashell with the guest's name written in gold would add interest. The pen can be found at a party or stationery store.

1. Fit the oasis inside the shallow dish. A pale, rose-colored dish works best. Place the candle on top of the foam.

Beeswax is preferred for its color, but an ordinary candle will do.

2. Stick the manzanita branches upright in the foam around the candle and pour sand to cover all of the oasis and the dish. Edge the sand on the table to suggest the curved line of a beach. Put sand candles in a triangular pattern outside of the dish and arrange seashells and coral around the candles, as well as around the branches.

3. On the fireplace mantel or a credenza, extend the decor using beeswax candles and bigger shells than those in the table setting.

Following are the materials needed to make sand candles:

- wet sand in 3"-deep cake pan or other flat container
- paraffin and candle wick
- double boiler
- 4" jar or container to create desired candle shapes
- $\frac{1}{2}$" metal washer

While the paraffin is melting in the double boiler, press the jar into the wet sand to make a candle mold.

Tie the metal washer onto the end of the wick and put the washer in the bottom of the candle mold. Tie the other end of the wick to a stick and put the stick down so it rests across the top of the pan holding the sand. Pour melted paraffin into the mold and let it harden. Cut the wick to $\frac{1}{2}$-inch and remove the candle from the sand.

BASIL OIL

2 bunches basil leaves
1 cup olive oil
ice water

Blanch basil leaves in boiling water for 15 seconds. Drain and transfer to ice water. Remove and squeeze excess water out of leaves. Put leaves and olive oil into blender and puree. Let stand overnight if possible. Strain through cheesecloth and reserve.

GARLIC CHIPS

8 cloves garlic
1½ cups milk
1 cup canola oil

Slice garlic cloves lengthwise, very thinly. Bring milk to a boil in small saucepan. Add garlic cloves and cook for 2 minutes. Strain out garlic and rinse under cold running water. Spread out garlic on paper towels and pat dry.

In a small saucepan, heat oil to 375 degrees. Fry garlic slices until golden brown, 5 to 15 seconds. Drain on paper towels and reserve.

To Serve: In a bowl, mix Niçoise vegetables with ½ of the balsamic vinaigrette and season with salt and pepper. Dress arugula with some of the remaining vinaigrette and season with salt and pepper.

Heat a skillet over high heat. Lightly oil tuna, season with salt and pepper and sear medallions on both sides, leaving tuna very rare in the center.

Spoon approximately ¼ cup Niçoise vegetables in a thin ring toward outer edge of each plate. Put 3 small spoonfuls of tapenade at triangle points on Niçoise vegetables. Place a small handful of arugula leaves in the center of each plate. Sprinkle garlic chips on arugula.

Place 2 seared tuna medallions on each plate in between tapenade points. Drizzle basil oil on tuna and around the plate. Serve immediately.

CRÈME BRULÉE

3 cups whipping cream
3 cups milk
1 cup sugar
1 vanilla bean, split and scraped
1 cinnamon stick
14 egg yolks
6 Tbs. brown sugar

Pre-heat oven to 300 degrees. In a heavy saucepan, bring whipping cream, milk, ½ cup sugar, vanilla bean and cinnamon stick to a boil. Let simmer for 5 minutes. Remove from heat and cover.

In a stainless steel bowl, whisk together egg yolks and remaining ½ cup sugar until mixture is pale and thickened. Using whisk, add cream and sugar mixture. Strain into a pitcher.

Divide strained custard among six ramekins. Place in a roasting pan. Fill with hot water halfway up the side of the ramekins, creating a water bath. Place roasting pan in oven and bake until just set, approximately 1 hour. Remove ramekins and refrigerate.

To Serve: Pre-heat broiler. Sprinkle each custard with 1 tablespoon brown sugar and broil until sugar melts and turns golden brown. Serve immediately.

PACIFIC RIM CONTEMPORARY DINNER FOR SIX

Featuring Elka Gilmore, Elka
San Francisco, California

Lobster with Coconut and Fava Beans

*"I hope
the passion
for what I do
is evident."*
—Elka Gilmore

E lka Gilmore treads a fine line between the conservative dictates of Georges Auguste Escoffier and her own impulse to revel in the flavors and ingredients of Asian cookery. The executive chef and creative force of Elka in San Francisco's Japan Town draws on French technique in her preparation and a Japanese aesthetic about food in her presentation. She demonstrates an unmitigated attention to detail, whether she is concentrating on technique or presentation of a dish.

~ MENU ~

Carpaccio of Striped Bass,
Ossetra Caviar and Ginger Vinaigrette

Napa Valley Sparkling Wine

Lobster with Coconut and Fava Beans

Robert Mondavi Carneros Chardonnay

Filet Mignon with Shiitake-Potato Galette
Tomato-Ginger Jam and Red Wine Sauce

Robert Mondavi Napa Valley
Cabernet Sauvignon Reserve

Chocolate Sushi

Robert Mondavi Napa Valley
Cabernet Sauvignon Reserve

Franco-Japanese is how Gilmore describes her cooking style. But while she derives inspiration from both French and Japanese traditions, the interpretation is hers. Her signature dishes have won her praise among San Francisco's knowledgeable restaurant clientele. It has won her influence among Americans who are showing interest increasingly in East-West cooking, a trend that is focused in California, but especially in San Francisco, gateway to the Pacific Rim.

With experience cooking on both coasts and in America's midland, this Texas-born chef arrived in San Francisco via Wisconsin, Massachusetts, France and, finally, Los Angeles.

At age 14, she managed to convince a restaurant to employ her. She had moved herself from Texas to Madison, Wisconsin, where her father lived. By the time she was 17, she was cooking at L'Etoile, one of Madison's finer restaurants, and studying chemistry at the University of Wisconsin. She participated in an accelerated study program and graduated at age 18.

She then headed East "to learn a few things." In Massachu-

setts, she met Marsha Sands, the owner of a seafood house. There, Gilmore cooked during the summer months. The rest of the year, she traveled and apprenticed in Europe. Her experience in the South of France "brought together the reason anybody ever envisioned an emulsified butter sauce," she says.

In 1982, she joined Sands in opening Camelions, a seafood restaurant in Los Angeles. Her menu of New England and French food with light Italian accents gave way to Tex-Mex in 1989, when she opened her own restaurant, Tumbleweed. She also owned and operated a wholesale seafood supply house.

Gilmore was writing her own culinary signature. It was not yet refined, but she was becoming increasingly independent of short-lived, popular strains in America's developing food craze. Her signature was becoming fresh seafood, organic produce and innovative pairings of taste and texture.

At the core, two principles remained: Remember Escoffier, and pay attention to the details of preparation: To enjoy the aesthetic of food, freshness and food texture are important, but so is composition on the plate.

Consider one of her chicken dishes. First, she marinates the chicken, following French technique. Then she cooks it on a flat-top griddle, weighted so the skin turns crispy. She serves it with the classic Japanese combination of braised bamboo shoots, fresh peas and onion juice. "I use very little butter, and the aesthetic of the food is quite elegant," says Gilmore.

It was her time in the wholesale seafood business that taught Gilmore what she describes as a "kinesthetic sense" for culling out the best and freshest fish. The rest she learned—and keeps on learning—by doing it her way. "Anybody can throw a piece of fish on the grill, but very few can touch a piece of fish and know how it needs to be cooked, at what temperature and with what flavors."

In Los Angeles, Gilmore started the Los Angeles Women's Culinary Alliance to promote the education of women in the restaurant industry.

After moving to San Francisco, she helped found the International Association of Women Chefs and Restaurateurs with a mandate to support women in the food service industry. "There still is tremendous discrimination against women," says Gilmore. "Real progress will come only when there isn't a gender associated with the word 'chef' and when women chefs no

Flowers and candlelight announce a menu that rivals the theatre for drama.

longer are lumped together because they are women."

Fond of wearing a baseball cap instead of a chef's toque, Gilmore enjoys acclaim for her definitive seafood at Elka, which opened in 1992. She likes cooking eel and black bass rather than swordfish and salmon. She prefers cooking on a stove to the fire of a grill. And she enjoys making sauces. "To me, roux is not a four-letter word."

For Gilmore, both the Japanese and the French cultures demonstrate a reverence for food that is missing in the United States. The Japanese have their tea ceremony, where tradition and aesthetics circumscribe each step. The French honor their chefs, going back to Escoffier, who was awarded the Légion d'Honneur in 1920, and who was made an Officer of the Order in 1928.

"In the United States, it still is much more a matter of eating to live, instead of living to eat. Although I think we are making great strides," says Gilmore.

Enjoying Wines Throughout the Meal

To enjoy wine with a meal, it is a simple matter to open a bottle and pour a glass, says Margrit Biever, vice president of cultural affairs the Robert Mondavi Winery. But attention to a few finer points increases the pleasure.

It is especially useful to have a sense about the serving order of wines whenever several wines are planned with a meal.

While there are many types of wine with such a range in taste, aroma and body, wine may be divided into three basic categories: appetizers, table wines, and desserts. Typically, they are served in that order.

Appetizer or aperitif wines are served before a meal to stimulate the appetite. Usually, these wines are dry. They include crisp Fumé Blancs or Sauvignon Blancs, and sparkling wines or Champagne.

Table wines are enjoyed with the meal. They include white, red, sparkling and rosé or

Margrit Biever

blush wines.

Generally speaking, it is best to start with light and delicate wines and progress to the more intense, full-bodied wines.

By following this order, a tendency is avoided for light wines to taste thin or watery after a rich, complex wine. It also is best to move from younger to older wines.

Dessert wines are sweet and full-bodied and are served after a meal. They may accompany sweets, fruit and cheese, but it is helpful to try to match the

intensity of the dessert's sweetness with the sweetness of the wine. Sweet wines bring out the fruitiness in food. However, the sweeter the dessert, the greater the chance it will overpower the wine, making it taste somewhat bitter.

Serving temperature of wine is a matter of individual taste. Tradition has it that both red and white wines are served at "room" temperature. But in this case, the room most often was in a drafty chateau with no central heating and air conditioning.

Ideally, serving temperatures for both red and white wines range from 55 to 65 degrees. An overly chilled white wine will numb taste buds and inhibit both the wine's character and expression of its aromas and flavors. Red wines should be served slightly cooled.

Once a bottle of wine is opened and exposed to air, the wine's sudden contact with oxygen causes the release of its bouquet. Letting wine breathe before serving gives the wine opportunity to "open up". Fresh, young wines or wines with a lighter style don't require breathing. In fact, it is not mandatory that any wine receive this treatment.

But if it is decided that a wine would benefit from breathing, there are several methods that can help the wine along. A widely used practice is simply to uncork the bottle one-half hour or so before serving. Speedier aeration can be achieved by pouring the wine into a glass and letting it stand, or by swirling the wine in the glass to release the aromas.

It is not uncommon to notice a changed bouquet each time the glass is swirled. The wine is developing new flavors as it breathes.

CARPACCIO OF STRIPED BASS, OSSETRA CAVIAR AND GINGER VINAIGRETTE

STRIPED BASS AND CAVIAR

6	2½ oz. pieces fresh striped bass fillet, boneless and skinless
1	Tbs. shallots, finely chopped
1	Tbs. chives, finely chopped
1	Tbs. English cucumber, peeled, seeded and finely diced
2	oz. ossetra caviar
	salt and white pepper

GINGER VINAIGRETTE

½	cup canola oil
1	tsp. grated ginger
¼	cup rice wine vinegar
1	tsp. shallots, finely chopped

Whisk together all ginger vinaigrette ingredients in a stainless steel bowl. Reserve.

With meat mallet, gently pound each piece of striped bass between 2 layers of plastic wrap until very thin and transparent. Remove plastic wrap and trim to fit inside rim of plates.

To Serve: Place "carpaccio" onto chilled plates. Sprinkle with shallots, chives and cucumber. Season with salt and white pepper. Drizzle with vinaigrette and dot all over with caviar. Serve immediately.

LOBSTER WITH COCONUT AND FAVA BEANS

LOBSTER

4	1½ lb. live Maine lobsters

Pre-heat oven to 450 degrees. Season and roast lobsters for 3 to 5 minutes. Take from oven and allow to cool slightly. Remove tail and claw meat carefully. Cut tail meat into medallions. Reserve warm.

SAUCE

2	Tbs. fresh basil, chopped
2	Tbs. fresh mint, chopped
2	Tbs. green onions, chopped

Carpaccio of Striped Bass with Caviar and Vinaigrette

2	Tbs. unsalted butter
1	Tbs. shallots, chopped
1¼	cup unsweetened coconut milk
1	Tbs. ginger juice (available at Asian markets)
¼	tsp. 7-pepper spice (available at Asian markets)
1	cup morel mushrooms, chopped
3	cups shelled fava beans (4-5 lbs., unshelled)
½	tsp. salt
1	lime, juiced
	chervil sprigs for garnish

In a small bowl, combine basil, mint and green onions. Reserve. Heat butter in a large skillet. Add shallots and sauté briefly. Add coconut milk, ginger juice, 7-pepper spice and morels, and reduce slightly. Add fava beans, herb and onion mixture and lime juice, and cook for about 2 minutes longer, until fava beans are tender. Adjust seasoning. Reserve warm.

To Serve: Divide fava bean mixture among 6 warm plates and arrange sliced lobster tail and claws in a circular mound. Garnish with chervil sprigs. Serve immediately.

FILET MIGNON WITH SHIITAKE-POTATO GALETTE TOMATO-GINGER JAM AND RED WINE SAUCE

FILET MIGNON

2	lbs. beef tenderloin, trimmed of all fat and sinew and cut into medallions

RED WINE SAUCE

1½	cups Robert Mondavi Cabernet Sauvignon
4	shallots, peeled and sliced
1	bay leaf
4	sprigs fresh thyme
½	tsp. black peppercorns, cracked
2½	cups rich beef stock
4	Tbs. unsalted butter
	salt and pepper

In a heavy saucepan, combine the red wine, shallots, bay leaf, thyme and peppercorns. Reduce over high heat to ¼ cup. Add the beef stock and continue to reduce until the sauce coats the back of a wooden spoon. Strain through a fine strainer and return to saucepan. Reserve.

SHIITAKE-POTATO GALETTE

1	lb. shiitake mushrooms, stemmed and sliced
5	Tbs. unsalted butter
3	Tbs. olive oil
2	large yellow onions, thinly sliced
8	medium russet potatoes, peeled and thinly sliced
	salt and pepper

Pre-heat oven to 375 degrees. Sauté the mushrooms in 2 tablespoons olive oil and 2 tablespoons butter over high heat until crisp. Season with salt and pepper. Reserve. Sauté onions over medium heat in 1 tablespoon olive oil and 1 tablespoon butter until tender. Season with salt and pepper. Combine with mushrooms and reserve.

Put one layer of sliced potatoes in bottom of 9-inch non-stick pan. Dot with remaining softened butter. Season with salt and pepper. Repeat process, adding 2 more layers of potatoes. Next add layer of mushroom/onion mixture, using all the mixture.

Finish with 3 more layers of potatoes, lightly seasoning each layer. Cover with foil and put weights on top. Bake for 50 to 55 minutes. Reserve.

TOMATO-GINGER JAM

5	Tbs. sugar
2	Tbs. ginger, peeled and finely minced
2	large tomatoes, peeled, seeded and cut into ½" dice
4	Tbs. unseasoned rice wine vinegar
	salt and pepper

Caramelize sugar in heavy saucepan over low heat. Add ginger and tomatoes and continue to cook over low heat until juices evaporate and jam thickens. Carefully stir in rice wine vinegar. Season with salt and pepper. Reserve.

To Serve: Grill or roast the medallions of filet mignon to desired doneness. Bring the reserved red wine sauce to a boil and whisk in the 4 tablespoons of butter. Season with salt and pepper.

Serve medallions with a wedge of potato galette and garnish with tomato-ginger jam. Nap with red wine sauce and serve immediately.

CHOCOLATE SUSHI

RICH CHOCOLATE SPONGE ROLL

8	egg whites
¾	cup sugar
1	cup all-purpose flour
½	tsp. baking powder
½	cup unsweetened cocoa powder
8	egg yolks
2	Tbs. unsalted butter, melted and cooled to room temperature
2	cups ginger snap cookies, coarsely pulverized
	spray release
	parchment paper

Whip egg whites to soft peaks. Add ½ the sugar and continue to whip until stiff and glossy. Transfer to a large mixing bowl. Sift together flour, baking powder and cocoa powder. Reserve. Whisk the egg yolks and remaining sugar together until thickened and pale yellow.

Simple Strokes Create Illusion of Drama

Flowers, round mirrors and candlelight are integral to the elegance that graces the center of the table and complements a dinner that is memorable in both taste and presentation. Drama is accomplished in a simple stroke in gold, black and white, using exotic flowers, black candles and a can of spray paint. These are the materials for the Pacific Rim dinner centerpiece:

- 18" round mirror; two 4" round mirrors
- 4", 6" and 8" black plastic trays
- 5" and 1" gold plastic risers
- 3 floral frogs
- bamboo and ruscus spray-painted in gold
- white roses, freesia and ixia
- star-of-Bethlehem
- Phalaenopsis orchid buds
- horsetail and Ming fern
- frosted candlesticks, 3 different heights
- 12" black candles
- several votive candle holders and candles

If substituting garden-variety flowers and a different color in candles, take care to provide for consistency in your theme. Above all, do not forgo the candles. The glow of soft candlelight enhances the enjoyment of dinner any time, any place.

1. The large mirror goes in the center of the table. The 8-inch black plastic tray is placed off-center on the 18-inch round mirror. The 6-inch tray is placed on a 1-inch riser, and the 4-inch tray is put on a 5-inch riser. Put 4-inch round mirrors in the plastic trays. Both, in turn, are put on the large, round mirror. (A dish turned upside down can substitute for a riser.)

2. One floral frog, plus water, goes in each tray to hold the flowers. Start with a stem of bamboo and ruscus in each frog, followed by 3 stems of horsetail, cut at different heights, 4 white roses per frog, 3 freesia per frog, 3 star-of-Bethlehem per frog, and 2 stems of ixia per frog. Each stem should be cut at different heights to create interest around the flowers.

Use the Ming fern, which is light and has an Asian look to it, to cover the frogs. As a final touch, float Phalaenopsis orchid buds in each tray.

3. Arrange the black candles in frosted candlesticks in a triangular pattern on the large, round mirror. Place the votive candles around the mirror.

Fold half of egg yolk mixture into egg whites. Fold in flour/cocoa mixture, then remaining egg yolk mixture. Finally, pour melted butter around outside edge of sponge batter and gently fold in.

Lightly coat the bottom of a baking sheet with spray release. Line the pan with parchment paper. Spray parchment with pan release. Spread batter evenly over parchment. Bake for 8 to 10 minutes until sponge just springs to the touch and is very moist. Remove from oven and invert while still hot onto another piece of parchment. Roll up like a jelly roll with parchment and allow to cool.

Carefully unroll cooled sponge and remove parchment. Spread a generous layer of dark chocolate ganache (recipe follows) over entire surface. With pastry bag fitted with large, open tip, pipe 1-inch-thick layer of chilled white chocolate ganache (recipe follows) over 1/3 of area and down the long side. Re-roll the "sushi" and cover the outside with dark chocolate ganache. Roll in crushed ginger snaps and refrigerate at least 1 hour.

DARK CHOCOLATE GANACHE

12	oz. bittersweet chocolate
9	Tbs. unsalted butter
3	Tbs. corn syrup
2	cups whipping cream
1/4	cup unsweetened cocoa powder

Over a double boiler, melt chocolate, butter and corn syrup. In heavy saucepan, add cocoa powder to cream and scald. Whisk into melted chocolate. Cool to room temperature. Reserve.

WHITE CHOCOLATE GANACHE

8	oz. white chocolate
2	Tbs. unsalted butter
1/2	cup whipping cream
2	tsp. orange zest, finely minced
2	Tbs. candied ginger, minced

Over a double boiler, melt chocolate with butter and cream. Whisk to incorporate completely. Refrigerate. When firm, stir in zest and ginger. Reserve.

MANGO-GINGER SAUCE

2	mangoes, peeled, pitted and pureed
1	tsp. ginger, peeled and grated
1/2	orange, juiced
	sugar to taste

In a stainless steel mixing bowl, whisk together mangoes, ginger and orange juice. Sweeten to taste with sugar. Refrigerate.

To Serve: Slice chocolate sushi on the diagonal into 4-inch-high portions. Place in centers of 6 plates, surround with mango-ginger sauce and serve immediately.

Hollywood Dinner Party for Four

Featuring Hans Röckenwagner, Röckenwagner and Fama
Los Angeles, California

Fresh Berry Gratin and Almond Croquant Parfait

Hans Röckenwagner enjoys breaking stereotypes. Just when he is about to be pinned down, this entrepreneurial chef pushes back professional barriers and beckons success to follow him once again. From a meager beginning in Venice Beach, Röckenwagner is now the owner of two successful restaurants in the glitzy, but oh, so competitive Los Angeles market.

One carries his name, Röckenwagner. The other he calls Fama, which he opened to accommodate his sister and her chef husband after they arrived in Los Angeles from the Röckenwagner

~ MENU ~

White and Green Asparagus,
Tobiko Caviar Vinaigrette

Red Bell Pepper Potato and Corn Risotto

Robert Mondavi Napa Valley Fumé Blanc

Roast Pork Tenderloin with Goat Cheese,
Garlic Flan, Smoked-Tomato Fondue
and Basil Oil

Robert Mondavi Carneros Pinot Noir

Fresh Berry Gratin, Almond Croquant Parfait

Robert Mondavi Moscato d'Oro

---

home in southern Germany.

Verve describes his menus. One food critic coined "Röck-enwagnerian" to illustrate both the whimsy and drama which distinguish his food. Finely diced potatoes replace rice in his risotto. Pork is paired with goat cheese and smoked tomato fondue in a slight alteration of the combination-made-in-heaven, goat cheese, tomato and basil. His berry and nougat parfait is an explosive taste experience.

When white asparagus is on the menu, Röckenwagner harks back to his German roots to provide a taste experience that belongs to Europe's rites of spring. Even his preparation draws on tradition. He personally takes charge of preparing the vegetable, even peeling it, which is a task typically left to kitchen apprentices. Just as each stalk must be shaved properly, the growing of white asparagus requires special attention. It must be dug up before it can sprout above the earth. Otherwise, its white color turns purple, then green.

The dish is finished in an operatic flourish with a dash of Tobiko caviar.

Röckenwagner's responsibilities extend to several employ-ees, including a master baker who arrived from Germany to oversee the chef's bakery business. It now operates seven days a week and is part of Röckenwagner in Santa Monica. Four bakers service wholesale accounts and supply Röckenwagner's restaurants.

What's ahead? Professionally, Röckenwagner hopes to be part-owner in a business that oversees a number of menus, all the while adhering to the quality that has brought success to Röckenwagner and Fama.

Röckenwagner's engaging entrepreneurial spirit has guided him in one professional decision after another, starting with his early days in southern Germany and continuing through his move to the bustling Midwest and finally to Los Angeles.

At age 15, Röckenwagner decided to escape his parents' restaurant in Schliegen and apprentice at the Zum Adler in Weil am Rhein. "It was boot camp," he says. By the time he left, he understood the value of endurance in the face of tough times. "The owner always said, 'If you can make it through my restaurant, you can make it anywhere.'"

It is unlikely, though, that the owner of Zum Adler foresaw the career path stretching out before this young, adventurous chef. While working as a short-order cook in an Alpine ski resort, Röckenwagner met the chef at one of Europe's grand hotels, the Beau-Rivage Palace, in Lausanne, Switzerland. He accepted an offer to jointly open La Grappe d'Or.

In 1982, Röckenwagner left for Paris, only to return later and encounter the owner of a Chicago restaurant. "He left behind a plane ticket with the offer, 'This is how much I will pay you. I want you to come and work for me.'" It took young Röckenwagner a week to decide. He arrived in Chicago, spent a year there and re-discovered his entrepreneurial spirit. When the restaurant closed, Röckenwagner decided to try Los Angeles.

It was 1984. He had little cash and the stubborn belief that the booming Los Angeles market offered promise. He reviewed 250 properties, settling on a run-down building on a crime-ridden street in Venice Beach. He turned the space into a cozy hole-in-the-wall. Success was his overnight.

By 1991, he had outgrown Röckenwagner in Venice Beach and moved to Main Street in Santa Monica. Röckenwagner now operates there in a complex designed by Frank Gehry, surrounded by chic boutiques and near the Santa Monica Museum of Fine Art.

Candlelight, glass and mirrors set the stage for a glittery dinner party featuring Roast Pork Tenderloin accompanied by Red Bell Pepper Potato and Corn Risotto.

WHITE AND GREEN ASPARAGUS, TOBIKO CAVIAR VINAIGRETTE

ASPARAGUS

8	large Belgian endive leaves
8	medium green asparagus
8	medium white asparagus
1	Tbs. sugar
½	tsp. salt

Cut all asparagus tips 1½ inches long. Bring 2 quarts water to a boil in a saucepan. Add green asparagus tips and cook 45 seconds. Place directly into ice water to cool. Remove from ice water, pat dry and reserve.

Bring 1 quart water to a boil with sugar and salt. Add white asparagus tips and cook 2 minutes. Remove pot from stove and let asparagus cool in the cooking liquid. Reserve.

The Rewards of Aging Fine Wines

The ancients had no choice but to drink their wine rough and ready, fresh from fermentation. In a notable advance, the Greeks made simple yet beautiful earthenware amphorae to store their wine.

Much later, wooden casks were used because they permitted just the right amount of oxygen to permeate the grain. Oak cooperage, developed by French and German winemakers in the Middle Ages, both protected wine from oxidation and allowed it to undergo subtle changes, which, over time, enhanced its natural goodness.

In the 17th century, winemakers understood the special synergy that exists between barrel, bottle and cork, and at last were ready to develop wines to their full maturity.

Today, we take the same pleasure as the ancients did in new wine.

But beyond the immediacy of the pleasure from drinking wine fresh from fermentation, there is delight in knowing that wine, especially certain varietals, improves with age.

Like a fine antique, a wine's character evolves. In this respect, it is a rare and wonderful exception among food products. No small wonder that a mystique has developed around the concept of wine aging in wine cellars.

The changes taking place both in the barrel and in the bottle during the aging process are complex. Minerals from the soil, vanillin from oak, hard and soft tannins, pigments, grape acids, esters and aldehydes react when exposed to oxygen and to each other along a continuum that winemakers refer to as a "marriage."

As in a marriage between two people, it is important to discourage the cropping up of negatives while simultaneously encouraging all that is best and harmonious for all involved.

Winemakers are stewards with responsibility for guiding their wines to maturity prior to bottling. At home, consumers are stewards too, protecting their wine to more thoroughly enjoy the benefits of aging. Above all, wine must be stored properly to fully develop over time. It needs darkness, a cool and even temperature, and only minimal, if any, vibration.

It is a source of pleasure to own several bottles of a favorite wine and to drink it at various times during the year or over the years. This is the way to enjoy the aging process of wine.

Many fine, naturally balanced Napa Valley and California wines will benefit from extended aging, although natural farming and advanced viticultural techniques also allow these wines to be enjoyed at the time of their release.

Patience of the wine lover — as with every aspect of the wine-making cycle—has its own very special rewards.

VINAIGRETTE

1	Tbs. red wine vinegar
2	Tbs. balsamic vinegar
¼	cup extra-virgin olive oil
2	Tbs. cooked egg white, finely chopped
2	Tbs. Tobiko caviar
1	Tbs. chives, finely minced
1	Tbs. sugar
½	tsp. salt

salt and white pepper

In a stainless steel bowl, combine vinegars and season with salt and pepper to taste. Slowly whisk in olive oil to form an emulsion.

Stir in cooked egg white, caviar, chives and sugar.

To Serve: Place one green and one white asparagus in the base of each endive leaf. Spoon 1 teaspoon of vinaigrette over asparagus and serve.

RED BELL PEPPER POTATO AND CORN RISOTTO

RISOTTO

2	cups russet potatoes, peeled and cut into ¼" dice
1	cup fresh corn kernels, approximately 1 ear
3	cups red bell pepper juice, approximately 8 bell peppers (recipe follows)
1	tsp. Hungarian paprika
¼	tsp. cayenne pepper
½	lemon, juiced
2	Tbs. whipping cream
¼	cup freshly grated Parmesan cheese
4	Tbs. unsalted butter
1	tsp. salt
¼	tsp. freshly ground white pepper

sprigs of chervil for garnish

In a 2-quart saucepan, reduce red bell pepper juice by ½. Add potatoes, corn kernels, paprika and cayenne. Cook over medium heat, stirring until potatoes are just tender and juice is reduced by an additional ⅓.

Add lemon juice and bring to a boil. Add heavy cream, re-

Pork Tenderloin with Goat Cheese, Tomato Fondue, Basil Oil and Garlic Flan

duce heat to a simmer and continue to cook until slightly thickened and creamy. Stir in Parmesan cheese and butter. Season with salt and white pepper to taste.

RED PEPPER JUICE

8	red bell peppers

Remove stems and seeds from peppers. Chop coarsely. Put peppers in food processor and puree. Transfer puree to a blender and liquefy, then strain through a fine strainer. (A vegetable juicer also can be used.)

To Serve: Garnish with chervil sprigs.

ROAST PORK TENDERLOIN WITH GOAT CHEESE, GARLIC FLAN, SMOKED-TOMATO FONDUE AND BASIL OIL

PORK TENDERLOIN

3	12-oz. pork tenderloins, cleaned of fat and sinew
8	oz. log of Montrachet goat cheese

salt and freshly ground black pepper

olive oil for frying

Slice each tenderloin into 4 equal pieces and pound lightly to form medallions approximately 2 inches in diameter and 2 inches thick. Reserve.

Cut log of goat cheese into 12 ¼-inch slices, using a cheese wire or fishing line. Reserve.

Pre-heat oven to 375 degrees. Heat 2 sauté pans over medium heat until hot. Add 1 tablespoon olive oil to each pan.

Season medallions with salt and pepper. Sear medallions on each side for approximately 2 minutes.

Place a slice of goat cheese on top of each medallion and put pans in oven for 10 minutes for medium-to well-done pork.

GARLIC FLAN

½   cup garlic cloves, blanched
2   tsp. unsalted butter
6   shallots, sliced
1   cup white vermouth
1   cup whipping cream
3   whole eggs
     salt and white pepper

Pre-heat oven to 300 degrees. Place garlic cloves in a small saucepan and cover with water. Bring to a boil, strain off water, add more cold water, boil again and strain. Repeat process a total of three times. Reserve.

In a 2-quart sauce pot, melt butter and add shallots. Sweat until translucent. Add blanched garlic and vermouth and reduce until almost dry. Add whipping cream, bring to a boil and season generously with salt and pepper. Puree in a blender until smooth. Strain through a fine mesh strainer and cool. Whisk eggs together and add to garlic cream.

Pour garlic cream into 4 buttered, 3-ounce soufflé molds. Place molds in a pan filled with hot water to cover ¾ of the way up the side of molds. Place in oven for 40 to 50 minutes or until a knife inserted in the center comes out clean. Remove and re-serve.

SMOKED-TOMATO FONDUE

10   Roma tomatoes, smoked*
1   Tbs. garlic, chopped
1   Tbs. shallots, chopped
½   bay leaf
2   Tbs. olive oil
6   sprigs fresh thyme
     salt and freshly ground white pepper

*To create a stove-top smoker:
1   disposable aluminum roasting pan,
     11" x 16" x 3"
1   cooling rack, 8" x 12"
     aluminum foil
     wood chips, approximately 1 cup

Spread wood chips over bottom of aluminum roasting pan. Put a 9" x 15" rectangle of foil over the chips, leaving a 1-inch border to allow smoke to escape. Place the cooling rack on top of the foil.

Arrange 5 tomatoes evenly on the rack. Cover and seal roasting pan with foil. Place on top of stove over medium heat. The chips will start to burn almost immediately. The smoke cooks and flavors the tomatoes in 10 minutes. Remove the tomatoes, peel and seed them. Reserve.

Bring a large pot of water to a rolling boil. Meanwhile, core remaining 5 tomatoes. Blanch for 10 seconds and immediately transfer to ice water. Peel, halve and seed the tomatoes.

Place fresh and smoked tomatoes in food processor and pulse until pureed but slightly chunky.

In a sauté pan, warm olive oil over medium heat. Add tomato puree, garlic, shallots and bay leaf. Cook slowly until thickened and juice has evaporated. Remove bay leaf, season with salt, pepper and fresh thyme. Reserve.

BASIL OIL

½   bunch fresh basil leaves
½   cup olive oil

Bring 2 quarts of water to a boil. Plunge basil leaves in water for 15 seconds and immediately drain and transfer to ice water. Remove and squeeze out excess water with your hands.

Place basil leaves in a blender with olive oil. Puree until very smooth. Put basil oil into clean container and let sit at room temperature overnight. Strain through a layer of cheesecloth. Reserve.

Make basil oil a day in advance. It will keep 3 to 5 days, covered, in a refrigerator.

Glitz and Glitter Brighten the Party

Invite guests to dress up as Hollywood stars and even tell them to come as Humphrey Bogart, Madonna, Oprah Winfrey or Denzel Washington. Meet their expectations for an evening of high-spirited entertainment with a party setting that is as glitzy and glittery as any Academy Awards party. Creating the ambience may take a little time, but it is well worth the kudos that will follow for days afterwards. Here is a list of the materials to recreate the centerpiece designed especially for Hans Röckenwagner:

- one 18" round ¼" mirror
- four 4" round ¼" mirrors
- one 12" and one 3" clear glass bubble vase
- one 15" x 4" clear glass cylinder vase
- about 1,000 clear glass marbles
- 3 glass candlesticks in different heights
- 3 12" candles
- 1 yard silver-wired ribbon
- 3 votive candle holders with candles
- 15 white tulips
- 3 purple anthurium
- 3 white and magenta dendrobium orchids
- optional: crystal ball or figurine

1. With a party setting that emphasizes glass, reflections and illusion, it's important to make sure that all materials are free of fingerprints. So, first wash all mirrors and glass objects. Now begin to create the atmosphere following this little rule: Stay off-center and decorate in odd-numbered configurations.

2. Place the large mirror in the center of the table and stack the 4-inch mirrors off-center on the large mirror. The reason for stacking the mirrors is to create a variety of heights, or pedestals, on top of the large center mirror.

3. Fill all glass vases 2 inches deep with marbles and add water to ½ inch above the marbles. In the 3-inch bubble vase, float 3 dendrobium orchids. In the cylinder vase, put 3 anthurium, cut to three different heights.

4. Cut the tulips to various heights. Starting with the shortest ones first, press them along the inside of the 12-inch bubble vase, creating an illusion of tulips painted on glass. Calla lilies also will work, although tulips are easier because their hollow stems mold more readily to the inside of the bowl.

5. After cutting the ribbon into 12-inch lengths, spiral one ribbon inside the glass cylinder. Loosely coil the remaining ribbon in a bubble vase. Arrange the candlesticks and votives in a triangular pattern and add the optional crystal ball or figurine.

To Serve: Remove and unmold a garlic flan onto the center of each plate. Place 1 tablespoon of smoked tomato fondue at 3 equidistant points outside the flan. Place one medallion of pork on each pool of tomato fondue. Garnish with drizzles of basil oil. Serve immediately.

FRESH BERRY GRATIN, ALMOND CROQUANT PARFAIT

ALMOND CROQUANT PARFAIT

3	oz. almonds, sliced and toasted
5	Tbs. granulated sugar
¾	cup powdered sugar
2	cups whipping cream
4	egg yolks
1	tsp. vanilla extract

Put granulated sugar in a heavy, 2-quart saucepan. Caramelize to a rich color by cooking carefully over medium heat. Stir in toasted almonds and remove from heat. Pour almond croquant onto a lightly oiled baking sheet and let cool until brittle. Once cool, remove from sheet and press into a fine meal, using a heavy knife. Reserve.

Place powdered sugar and egg yolks in a stainless steel bowl. Whisk vigorously over a pot of simmering water until thickened, 5 to 6 minutes. Remove from heat and let cool 5 minutes. In a separate bowl, whip the cream to soft peaks. Using a rubber spatula, gently fold the egg yolk mixture into the whipped cream. Then fold in the crushed croquant.

Line the bottom of an 8 x 8-inch baking pan with parchment paper. Pour parfait into pan. Freeze until firm.

WHIPPED SAUCE ANGLAISE

2	cups whipping cream
½	vanilla bean, split
5	egg yolks
5	Tbs. sugar

In a heavy saucepan, bring whipping cream and vanilla bean to a boil. Remove from heat, cover and steep for 10 minutes. In a stainless steel bowl, whisk egg yolks and sugar until pale and thickened. Slowly whisk hot cream into egg yolk mixture. Set custard over simmering water and stir continuously until it coats the back of a wooden spoon. Remove from heat, strain and cool. Whip cooled crème anglaise to soft peak stage and reserve.

FRUIT

16	fresh strawberries, thinly sliced
1½	cups fresh raspberries
1½	cups fresh blackberries

To Serve: Pre-heat broiler. Cut frozen parfait in 3 x 4-inch squares. Spread 4 tablespoons of whipped, cooled anglaise evenly over each of 4 ovenproof plates. One by one, place each plate under the broiler until anglaise sauce is golden brown. Place a slice of parfait in the center of each plate. Surround the parfait with sliced strawberries. Top with fresh raspberries and blackberries. Garnish with fresh mint and serve immediately.

SOUTHERN
LATE-AFTERNOON
JAZZ PARTY FOR TEN

Featuring David Danhi, Georgia
Los Angeles, California

Georgia's Peach Cobbler

"Mine is a '90s approach — geared toward healthy and fresh food."
—Dave Danhi

Georgia is an upscale Southern food restaurant on funky Melrose Avenue in Los Angeles. The menu is fried chicken, grits and collard greens cooked with Executive Chef Dave Danhi's zealous concern about cholesterol and fats. The restaurant's name is obviously Southern, although the chef grew up in Manhattan Beach and acquired his training in New York's Catskill Mountains and in Southern California. Contradictions abound, but so do good taste, high quality and comfort, all served up over Danhi's signature—a sophisticated take on Southern cooking with an emphasis on healthy food.

~ MENU ~

Black-Eyed Pea Tart

Georgia's Famous BBQ Ribs

Robert Mondavi Napa Valley Fumé Blanc

Crayfish-Stuffed Soft-Shell Crab Etouffée

Georgia's Famous Fried Chicken

Dirty Rice

Georgia's Mashed Potatoes

Collard Greens

Robert Mondavi Napa Valley Chardonnay

Georgia's Peach Cobbler

Robert Mondavi Napa Valley
Moscato d'Oro

When it comes to food, Danhi's approach tends in the direction of the '90s. Healthy is a key element in his emphasis on food that is fresh and organically produced.

As a consequence, Danhi cooks his collard greens with smoked turkey, not pork, which is the tradition in the South. If oil is called for, he uses olive oil. If food is fried, he uses canola oil. His crabcakes are a specialty, and for this dish he uses 100-percent Maryland blue crab. He will reject any crab that's been out of the water for more than three days.

The Southern spirit inspiring Danhi's menu came as a welcome surprise to the jaded Los Angeles palate. Danhi reports food sales in the 75-percent range, compared to the even split between food and beverage that is typical for restaurant sales.

An emphasis on Old South comfort, with indoor and outdoor seating, also adds to the atmosphere at the restaurant, which is owned by Norm Nixon, an ex-National Basketball Association star, movie stars Denzel Washington and Eddie Murphy, restaurateurs Brad Johnson and John Long, and record executive Lou Adler.

Danhi acquired his know-how about managing a restaurant during the five years he spent with the University Restaurant Group, owners of a half-dozen Southern California restaurants. There he learned about the financials, production, the need for freshness and the value of the rule: Quality first and everything else afterwards.

"It's not the chef who cooks everything. A lot of what I do involves overseeing the kitchen," says Danhi. The challenge is to keep a balance between the time it takes to "move it out" and to be creative. "I'm the type who says I will take the day off, but who ends up coming in and staying. It's a passion. You have to love this business to stay in it."

BLACK-EYED PEA TART

BLACK-EYED PEAS

1¼	cups black-eyed peas
1	qt. chicken stock
½	cup onion, finely chopped
¼	cup celery, finely chopped
2	Tbs. parsley, minced
1	bay leaf
2	tsp. garlic, minced
1	tsp. fresh thyme
2	tsp. lightly packed brown sugar
1	tsp. apple cider
½	cup smoked turkey, minced
¾	tsp. salt
1	tsp. Worcestershire sauce
1	Tbs. Tabasco sauce
1	tsp. beef base, optional
¼	tsp. each, black, white and cayenne peppers

In a large casserole, bring the peas to a strong boil for 5 minutes. Remove from heat and allow to stand for one hour. In a second casserole, bring all other ingredients to a boil in chicken stock. Reduce to a simmer. Drain the peas and add them to the broth. Reduce to a simmer and cook until peas are very soft. Add water if necessary to keep peas covered during this process. Drain and reserve. Return cooking liquid to a boil and reduce to about 1 cup. Return peas to the casserole and toss in reduced cooking liquid. Adjust seasoning and reserve.

❧ A Dave Danhi buffet extravaganza beckons guests to feast on taste and visual delights and to enjoy Robert Mondavi wines.

CORNMEAL PASTRY FOR TART SHELLS

2	cups cornmeal
2	cups flour
2	tsp. salt
4	tsp. baking powder
2	tsp. sugar
¾	cup butter
1½	cups whipping cream

Pre-heat oven to 350 degrees. Combine all dry ingredients in mixing bowl. Add butter and mix on low speed with paddle. Slowly add cream until mixture comes together and looks "sandy." Remove from bowl and divide into 2 parts. Shape dough into disks and cover with plastic. Chill.

Remove from refrigerator 1 hour before rolling out pastry to approximately ¼-inch thick. Cut into circles to fit 10 4 x 1-inch individual tart pans. Press into tart pans that are lightly greased, and bake until light golden brown. Remove from pans, cool and reserve.

To Serve: Pre-heat oven to 375 degrees. Fill cornmeal tart shells with black-eyed peas and bake for 6 to 7 minutes until hot. Serve immediately.

GEORGIA'S FAMOUS BBQ RIBS

BBQ RIBS

8	baby back pork ribs, 1½ lbs. each

RIB RUB

½	Tbs. cayenne pepper
1½	Tbs. salt

Picking the Glass is an Art

Wine is enjoyed with all the senses—sight, smell, taste, touch, and even sound when the glasses are clinked in a toast. In fact, fine wine glasses are designed to enhance the sensual experience of tasting wine.

Any glass will do, of course, but a proper glass enhances the pleasure the wine has to offer.

A good wine glass is thin, clear, colorless and stemmed. It is clear so the wine's color and clarity can be fully appreciated.

The stem allows the glass to be held without the hand touching the bowl and prematurely warming the wine.

Wine glasses also are curved slightly at the rim, which helps capture the wine's bouquet in the glass. In order for the wine to flow smoothly, the rim should be no thicker than the glass itself. The glass should be clean and free of any detergent residue. Off aromas can mar the finest wine.

A goblet bowl should hold at least 12 ounces or more and be large enough for swirling the wine without spilling it. This releases the aromas, or allows it to "breathe." White wines are best enjoyed in medium-sized bowls that hold at least 9 ounces and that help concentrate the bouquet in the glass. Long, tall flutes show off and conserve the stream of bubbles in Champagne or sparkling wines.

The world's finest crystal makers have engineered glasses that bring out the best qualities of individual wine varietals. The shape of the glass is important for controlling the flow of the wine to those parts of the tongue that register sweetness, saltiness, acidity and bitterness.

For example, properly designed crystal glass guides a Cabernet Sauvignon to the tongue's tip, where sweetness is accentuated. The theory is that the Cabernet's rich fruit will form the most lasting impression and the wine's acidity and tannin will be de-emphasized. The overall perception is of a smoother, rounder wine.

½   cup chili powder
¼   cup paprika
1½ Tbs. onion powder
1½ Tbs. garlic powder
¼   cup ground cumin
½   Tbs. white pepper
½   cup lightly packed brown sugar

Mix ingredients together. Reserve in air-tight container.

BBQ SAUCE

1   large onion, finely chopped
1   cup chutney
¼   cup Worcestershire sauce
6   Tbs. apple cider vinegar
¼   cup honey
¼   cup lightly packed, light brown sugar
1   tsp. salt
1   tsp. black pepper
1   tsp. white pepper
1   tsp. cayenne pepper
1½ tsp. ground dry mustard
½   cup butter
½   lemon, juiced
28 oz. bottled chili sauce
28 oz. ketchup
2   Tbs. Louisiana hot sauce

In a blender or food processor, puree onions with chutney until smooth. Transfer mixture to heavy saucepan. Add all remaining ingredients. Bring to a simmer over medium heat. Reduce heat and cook for 45 minutes, stirring occasionally.

Generously season both sides of ribs with Rib Rub. Preheat oven to 350 degrees. Place ribs in large, 2-inch-deep baking pan. Fill pan 1-inch deep with water. Cover with plastic wrap and then aluminum foil. Bake for 1½ to 2 hours, until meat pulls away from bone. Remove from oven and reserve.

To Serve: If a commercial smoker is available, follow manufacturer's directions. Otherwise, prepare grill using mesquite charcoal and hickory wood chips that have been soaked in water for 45 minutes. Grill ribs over hot coals until they begin to darken, turning often. Brush generously with BBQ sauce during last few minutes. Place on platter and serve immediately.

Crayfish and Soft-Shell Crabs

CRAYFISH-STUFFED SOFT-SHELL CRAB ETOUFFÉE

CRAYFISH AND SOFT-SHELL CRABS

48 live crayfish
20 live soft-shell crabs
2   cups all-purpose flour
1   cup unsalted butter
salt and pepper

Cook crayfish in boiling salted water for 5 minutes. Drain and cool. Remove tails and reserve.

With a very sharp knife or pair of scissors, remove the eyes and front ½-inch of the soft-shell crabs. Carefully lift the soft shell up and remove gills with the tip of a paring knife.

Season flour with salt and pepper. Dredge crabs in flour, shaking off excess. Heat large skillet over high heat. Add 3 tablespoons of butter. Sauté 3 or 4 crabs at a time, turning once, about 3 or 4 minutes per side until crispy. Pour off used butter and renew as necessary for remaining crabs. Season with salt and pepper. Reserve warm.

ETOUFFÉE

¾   cup unsalted butter
½   cup all-purpose flour

2	large onions, finely diced
3	Tbs. garlic, minced
4	jalapeño peppers, seeded and diced
6	celery stalks with leaves, finely diced
2	red bell peppers, seeded and finely diced
4	cups ripe tomatoes, diced
4	cups clam juice
4	tsp. tomato paste
4	tsp. Worcestershire sauce
2	lemons, juiced
1	tsp. fresh oregano, chopped
1	Tbs. fresh thyme, chopped
½	cup parsley, chopped
2	tsp. cayenne pepper
2	cups green onions, chopped
	salt and pepper

Melt butter in large, heavy sauté pan. Stir in the flour and cook over low heat to make dark brown roux. Stir often. Add onions, garlic, jalapeños, celery and bell peppers. Cook for 10 minutes, stirring often.

Add tomatoes and continue to cook for 10 more minutes. Add clam juice, tomato paste, Worcestershire sauce and lemon juice. Simmer for 15 to 20 minutes more. Add oregano, thyme, parsley, cayenne and green onions and continue to cook until mixture has thickened and most of the water has evaporated. Adjust seasoning. Stir in crayfish tails and cook to just heat through. Remove from heat and reserve.

To Serve: Bring the etouffée mixture back to a simmer. Check seasoning. Place crispy crabs on a large serving platter and smother with etouffée sauce. Serve immediately.

GEORGIA'S FAMOUS FRIED CHICKEN

CHICKEN

2	frying chickens, cut up
4	cups buttermilk
4	cups peanut oil, for frying

Pre-heat oven to 350 degrees. Pour buttermilk into large stainless steel bowl. Submerge chicken in buttermilk.

Heat oil to 375 degrees. Take one piece of chicken at a time from the buttermilk, drain off excess liquid and dredge in flour mixture (recipe follows). Carefully put chicken in hot oil. Working in small batches, repeat process with remaining chicken. Fry for approximately 10 minutes, depending on size of each piece. Place chicken on baking sheet and finish cooking in oven for 10 to 15 minutes. Reserve warm.

FRIED-CHICKEN FLOUR

2¾	cups all-purpose flour
6	Tbs. cayenne pepper
1½	Tbs. salt
½	Tbs. white pepper
½	Tbs. black pepper
¾	tsp. garlic powder
¾	tsp. onion powder
¾	tsp. poultry seasoning

In a large bowl, combine flour, cayenne, salt, white pepper, black pepper, garlic powder, onion powder and poultry seasoning. Reserve.

To Serve: Remove cooked chicken from oven, transfer to platter and serve.

DIRTY RICE

6	Tbs. butter
1½	cups onion, finely diced
1½	cups celery, finely diced
1½	cups red bell pepper, finely diced
1½	cups green bell pepper, finely diced
2	Tbs. garlic, minced
4½	cups white rice
½	Tbs. cayenne
1	Tbs. salt
2	Tbs. black pepper
3½	Tbs. paprika
3	Tbs. dry mustard
4	bay leaves
3	tsp. ground cumin
1½	tsp. dried thyme
1½	tsp. dried oregano
4	cups shrimp or chicken stock
2	cups water

Pre-heat oven to 350 degrees. In a large pot, sauté onion,

Make Party Decor Jazzy Too

Kick back, listen to the music and enjoy a buffet presented with a tantalizing decor that depends
on vegetables right out of the refrigerator. The objective is to make it easy for guests to mill
informally around an attractively set table, enjoying the food and each other's company.
Here are the necessary materials, although creative substitutions also will work:

- glazed pot filled with floral foam (oasis) and water
- 3 each, plum and pear branches with fruit
- 1 fig branch with fruit
- 3 miniature persimmon branches
- 3 blooming artichokes
- 1 bunch lavender
- 3 garden roses
- 3 stems each, allium, larkspur and drumstick
- 13 stems sprengeri fern
- 6 artichokes and 1 bunch radishes on bamboo skewers
- 3 eggplant, 5 garlic bulbs
- 7 artichokes, assorted sizes
- 2 bunches radishes, 1 bunch each, asparagus and red onions with greens

The objective is to create a cascade of vegetables that flows from the pot of flowers to the buffet platters. The vegetables should appear to be part of the decor.

1. Arrange the fruit branches, flowers and the skewered vegetables in the pot. (After the party, both the radishes and the artichokes can be eaten.)

2. Slide risers under the tablecloth to create different levels for the platters. The number of risers will depend on the number of platters needed for serving. After the platters are in place, bunch the excess tablecloth around the risers to "cloud" the area. That way, any food that is spilled during serving is caught in the folds.

3. Spread the fern around the platters and group the vegetables on the table.

celery, red and green bell peppers and garlic in butter for 3 minutes. Add rice and sauté 5 more minutes. Stir in remaining ingredients. Test for seasoning. The broth should taste a little salty. Bring to a boil, cover tightly and place in oven for 20 minutes. Remove from oven and allow to rest, partially uncovered, for 15 minutes before serving.

GEORGIA'S MASHED POTATOES

6½	lbs. Idaho potatoes
2½	cups whipping cream
1½	cups unsalted butter
⅓	cup sour cream
⅓	cup mayonnaise
	salt and white pepper

Peel and cube potatoes into 1-inch squares. Put potatoes in large casserole and cover with water. Bring to a boil over high heat. Reduce to a simmer and cook until tender. Do not over-cook or finished dish will taste watery.

Combine whipping cream and butter in another saucepan and simmer. Reduce by ¼. Reserve. Drain potatoes and allow to sit for 5 minutes to cool slightly. Place potatoes in bowl and whip with a hand-mixer until fluffy. Add sour cream, mayonnaise and ¾ of cream/butter mixture. Add rest of cream/butter mixture as needed to reach desired consistency. Season with salt and pepper. (Mashed potatoes can be held, covered, in a warm water bath for several hours.)

COLLARD GREENS

½	cup butter
3	onions, sliced
2	Tbs. garlic, minced
1½	cups smoked turkey, diced
4	Tbs. white vinegar
½	cup brown sugar
2	Tbs. chicken base (optional)
¾	tsp. white pepper
¾	tsp. black pepper
4	cups chicken stock
1	Tbs. fresh thyme
¾	tsp. cayenne pepper
3	Tbs. beef base
1	Tbs. salt
6	large bunches collard greens, coarsely chopped

Sauté onion and garlic in butter until soft. Add all remaining ingredients except greens. Bring to a boil and stir in greens. Cover and simmer over medium-high heat for 2½ hours, stirring occasionally. (This recipe is best when made a day ahead.)

GEORGIA'S PEACH COBBLER

COBBLER FILLING

5½	lbs. peaches, peeled and sliced
1½	cups sugar
1	cup lightly packed brown sugar
1½	tsp. cinnamon
1	tsp. nutmeg
½	tsp. ground ginger
1	Tbs. flour
½	tsp. salt
1	Tbs. orange juice
½	Tbs. lemon juice
3	Tbs. butter, melted
1	tsp. vanilla extract

In a large stainless steel bowl, combine all ingredients, except peaches, and mix well. Toss peaches in mixture. Reserve.

TOPPING

2	cups flour
1½	cups sugar
1	Tbs. baking powder
3	eggs

Pre-heat oven to 325 degrees. Combine all dry ingredients in a mixing bowl. Stir in eggs, one at a time, until pastry is well blended. Fill 10 6-ounce ramekins with peaches. Crumble topping evenly over peaches. Drizzle with melted butter and bake for approximately 1 hour or until golden brown.

To Serve: Present warm with vanilla ice cream.

POOLSIDE HAWAIIAN LUNCH FOR SIX

Featuring Alan Wong, Le Soleil
Kohala Coast Bay, Hawaii

Tropical Seafood Salad

Hawaiian legend has it that strength infuses the surroundings at Le Soleil restaurant. Part of Mauna Lani Bay Hotel and Bungalows, Le Soleil is where Alan Wong is re-defining one of America's popular regional cuisines. Prehistoric lava flows form the geological base for the resort's oceanfront property, a site which once served as the playground to none less than Hawaii's nobility. Renowned for its Kaláhuipuàa's fish ponds, legend has it that regal runners were employed to carry mullet and awa, still alive from the ponds, post-haste to the table of Chief Kamehameha, later King of the Hawaiian Islands.

~ MENU ~

New Wave Oyster Shooters
with Wasabi Pearl and Spiced Tomato Water

Chinese-Style Roast Duck
with Avocado Ginger Sake Salsa

"Ahi Cake" Layered with Grilled Eggplant,
Maui Onions and Vine-Ripened Tomatoes
Lemongrass Goat Cheese Dressing

Tropical Seafood Salad

Robert Mondavi Napa Valley Pinot Noir

Lychee Ginger Sorbet with Island Fruits

Robert Mondavi Moscato d'Oro

The islands' aristocracy has long since given way to a beautiful vacationland resort, but the spirit lingering behind the legend surfaces when Wong, of Japanese and Chinese Hawaiian descent, speaks of his commitment to excellence.

His is a commitment born of serendipitous opportunity to leave the small Hawaiian town of Wahiawa in the middle of pineapple fields for training at the posh Greenbrier Hotel in White Sulphur Springs, West Virginia, and later at New York's long-established house of classic French cuisine, Lutèce.

His early career path did not follow the upward progression so often anticipated by successful people. Zig-zags challenged him. He apprenticed at the Greenbrier, choosing on-the-job training over an expensive, New York culinary education. When he told his boss he was ready for New York, his boss laughed. When he told him he wanted to work at Lutèce, his boss laughed harder.

From Lutèce's owner, the best assurance he could glean was the mere prospect of employment. Back in Hawaii, Wong waited, only to return later to New York to work in another restaurant. Finally, in early 1983, Lutèce hired him. That was "the biggest blessing I've ever received," Wong says.

Wong's work at the Manhattan restaurant became the culinary foundation he relies on to this day. Specifically, its passion for culinary excellence continues to inspire him. His emulsified tarragon vinaigrette, which he uses in his tropical seafood salad, is made by following the classic French method. His Chinese-style roast duck and avocado combination was spurred by work he saw in Lutèce's kitchen.

While French basics inform his dishes, Wong's cookery explodes with flair, in taste and in presentation. His seafood salad draws on the Hawaiian staples of papaya, mango and avocado, which are served cold with warm, sautéed shrimp and lobster, plus a dab of garlic butter.

The finish on his duck and avocado combination happened by accident. While making a guest appearance, Wong by mistake added tapioca starch to the crepe batter. Since the first crepe routinely is discarded anyway, Wong tossed it in a deep fryer. It puffed up like a chip—and became an integral part of one of his signature dishes.

Wong refers to his work as "Hawaiian regional cuisine." It features the flavors of Hawaiian cookery—ginger, fish sauce and soy—and it reflects a classical training in French cookery as well as in the many cultures that are represented on the islands of Hawaii.

Wong seasons with the pungent wasabi, the green Asian horseradish paste; uses chile pepper water, made from chiles, garlic, ginger and vinegar, as a table condiment to replace salt and pepper; and relies on tomato water to add tartness or to thin out a dish.

His tomato water is the gift that comes of efficiency. Since the tomatoes he uses are expensive, Wong blends the trimmings to make a pulp, which is left overnight in a coffee filter. The result is a jazzy, versatile ingredient in a number of Wong's dishes.

Fame's spotlight turns Wong's way each summer when Cuisines of the Sun, sponsored by the Mauna Lani Bay resort for the nation's premier food writers, takes place. The food fair features menus that reflect cuisines from sunny climates. Both Wong's ahi cake and his lychee ginger sorbet are the result of presentations he made during the annual event on the big island of Hawaii.

*Alan Wong's luncheon fare and
Robert Mondavi wine await guests at poolside.*

AMERICA'S RISING STAR CHEF
ALAN WONG
Canoe House, Hawaii
Presents
Pool-Side Hawaiian Lunch for Six

New wave oyster shooters with a wasabi pearl
Spiced tomato water

Chinese-style Tombo ahi chuck slices
with avocado and sake salsa

"Ahi cake" layered with grilled eggplant
Maui onions and sun-ripened tomatoes
Lemongrass goat cheese dressing
Tropical green salad
Pinot

Lychee ginger sorbet with island fruits
Mescado oro

A graduate of the two-year culinary program at Honolulu's Kapiolani Community College, Wong is a chef of many strengths. He once dreamed of being a baseball coach. He has long since given up on the baseball diamond, but his dream infuses an important dimension of his work. Wong has a passion for passing on to others his knowledge about food.

"In my life, there have been many people who helped me get what I needed to do the work I do. Now I want to help young people find the opportunities they need to get ahead in life. Anybody can do this. It doesn't matter how much money you have or what color you are.

"What matters is that you want to do it badly enough," says Wong.

NEW WAVE OYSTER SHOOTERS WITH WASABI PEARL AND SPICED TOMATO WATER

SHOOTERS

6	fresh oysters
24	pieces green onion, sliced hair-thin on the diagonal
24	pieces tomatoes, diced small
6	Niçoise olives, pitted
12	thin slices fennel bulb
1½	tsp. ume (pickled plums), diced small
4	shiso leaves, very thinly sliced

Traditional Shapes and Colors of Wine Bottles

Wine has been an integral part of civilized life for some 7,000 years, but the glass wine bottle was not used widely until the late 18th century. This technical advancement revolutionized the quality and availability of wine.

Before the glass bottle, wine was stored in the container in which it was shipped — a fired clay jar, which the ancient Greeks called an amphora. Later, wooden barrels were used. The drawback of both the amphora and the barrel was that once either was opened, the remaining wine was subject to spoilage.

The impervious glass bottle, on the other hand, preserved the wine's flavor for longer periods of time and in smaller, more convenient amounts. The change in storage techniques also made it possible for more complex white and red wines to improve over time. Since glass does not interact with wine, the closed, clean environment that it provides allows wine to reach its optimum expression in complexity, balance and style.

As bottles became more commonplace, bottle shapes and colors became associated with different types of wine. Tradition has it that the straight-sided cylinder bottles with high shoulders, called "Bordeaux" bottles, hold red and white varietals which originated in France's Bordeaux region.

Cabernet Sauvignon and Merlot typically are stored in Bordeaux bottles, since these wines are made from the grapes grown principally in this region.

The softer-shouldered "Burgundy" bottles are used for Chardonnay and Pinot Noir. Johannisberg Riesling and Sylvaner, wines of Alsace and Germany, are stored in "Hock" bottles, which are tall and gracefully tapered bottles. The Champagne or sparkling wine bottle tends to have a shape that is similar to the Burgundy bottle, but heavier.

The majority of fine American wines are stored in bottles with these traditional European shapes. For example, most California Cabernet Sauvignons are found in a high-shouldered, dark green Bordeaux bottle with a punt or push-up indentation in the bottom of the bottle.

Various theories explain the reason for the punt. Some claim its purpose is to make the bottle stronger. Others argue that it collects sediment as the wine ages.

Color also is a distinctive feature of wine bottles. It was determined early on that light rays can harm a wine's flavor. Colored glass thus became important to protect wine from light damage, especially during the aging process.

Tradition also plays a role in the choice of glass color. Dark green is used for Cabernet Sauvignon, Zinfandel and Merlot. Lighter greens are used for Chardonnay, Pinot Noir and Chenin Blanc. Amber is associated with Rhine Valley wine bottles, and green or greenish blue with Moselle Valley bottles, both of Germany.

6 pieces basil leaf
6 chervil sprigs
6 pearl-sized balls of wasabi paste
¾ cup spiced tomato water (recipe follows)

TOMATO WATER

10 ripe Roma tomatoes, or equivalent

Blend ripe tomatoes or tomato scraps. Drain the pulp through a coffee filter for several hours or overnight to make tomato water or essence.

SPICED TOMATO WATER

1 cup tomato water
1 Tbs. chili pepper water (¼ tsp. red chili flakes in a cup of boiling water)
2 garlic cloves, thinly sliced
6 basil leaves, very finely diced
6 Tbs. fennel, thinly sliced
 salt and pepper

Combine ingredients in a bowl. Season with salt and pepper. Let sit in refrigerator for 1 hour to allow flavors to develop. Strain and reserve, chilled.

To Serve: Place green onion threads in the bottoms of tall, slender "shooter" glasses. Divide remaining dry ingredients, except chervil and wasabi pearls, between glasses. Take care not to compact the ingredients. They must exit the glass when the shooter is drunk. Fill with spiced tomato water. Garnish each with chervil sprig and a wasabi pearl. Serve immediately.

CHINESE-STYLE ROAST DUCK WITH AVOCADO GINGER SAKE SALSA

ROAST DUCK

2 duck breasts, skin on
1 tsp. 5-pepper spice (available in Asian markets)
 salt
 hoisin sauce (available in Asian markets)
 green onion, shredded for garnish

Pre-heat oven to 375 degrees. Score the skin side of the breasts with a sharp knife. Heat a non-stick skillet on medium heat. Cook the breasts skin side down until most of the fat is

New Wave Oyster Shooter

rendered and the skin is well colored. Remove from pan and pat dry with paper towel. Rub skin well with 5-pepper spice and season with salt. Roast breasts in oven for 15 minutes, skin side up. Remove and test for doneness. If the skin is not crispy, return to the skillet for a few minutes.

CHILI SCALLION CREPES

1 scant cup tapioca starch
¼ cup hot water
¼ cup half-and-half
1 egg
2 Tbs. flour
¼ cup green onion, sliced
½ tsp. cayenne pepper
½ tsp. salt
 peanut oil for frying

Combine all ingredients in a stainless steel bowl and mix well. Allow to sit refrigerated for at least 2 hours or overnight. Batter should be very thin. Use hot water to thin out if necessary.

Use 3 tablespoons batter for each crepe. Using a 7-inch non-stick crepe pan, make 8 or more very thin crepes. Cut each crepe into 8 wedges. Heat the oil to 375 degrees. Deep-fry the crepe wedges until they puff up. Drain and reserve.

AVOCADO GINGER SAKE SALSA

2	small avocados, finely diced
2	tomatoes, seeded and diced
1	small onion, finely minced
2	limes, juiced
1	small dry chili pepper
2	Tbs. sake
4	Tbs. canola oil
2	Tbs. cilantro, chopped
1	Tbs. green onion, finely sliced
1	Tbs. ginger, finely minced

Thoroughly combine ingredients. Refrigerate and reserve.

TARO CHIPS

3	fresh taro roots
	peanut oil for frying

Peel taro and slice as thinly as possible, preferably on a slicing machine. Heat oil to 375 degrees. Dry taro slices and deep-fry a few at time. Drain and reserve.

To Serve: Place a large tablespoon of salsa in the center of each plate. Arrange eight pieces of crepe around the salsa. Put a teaspoon of salsa on top of each crepe wedge. Next, put a thin slice of duck on each, then a dab of hoisin sauce. Garnish each duck slice with green onion threads. Serve with taro chips on the side.

AHI CAKE LAYERED WITH GRILLED EGGPLANT, MAUI ONIONS AND VINE-RIPENED TOMATOES LEMONGRASS GOAT CHEESE DRESSING

AHI CAKE

12	oz. Japanese eggplant
1	lb. Maui or other sweet onions
$2/3$	cup olive oil, infused with 2 garlic cloves
8	oz. ahi tuna, #1 sashimi grade
12	oz. ripe tomatoes, thinly sliced
$1/2$	oz. basil leaves
	sprigs of basil for garnish

Slice eggplant and onions into $1/4$-inch pieces. Place in a bowl, season with salt and pepper and let stand for 30 minutes. Pour off liquid and drizzle with $1/2$ cup infused olive oil. Grill eggplant and onions until fully cooked. Transfer to a baking sheet and refrigerate.

Cut tuna into $1/4$-inch slices. Season with salt and pepper. Use a small amount of olive oil to sear the tuna slices quickly on both sides in a hot skillet. Immediately refrigerate to stop cooking. Fish should be raw inside.

Line glass bowl with plastic wrap. Cover the bottom of the bowl with overlapping tomato slices. Layer onions, then basil, then eggplant in the bowl. Drizzle with 1 tablespoon of infused olive oil. Next, place a layer of ahi tuna slices over the vegetables. Tuna may have to be cut and pieced together to cover the vegetables.

Repeat this procedure, creating a second layer of vegetables, infused oil and seared tuna. For the last layer, reverse the order, ending up with tomato slices on top.

Cut a circular-shaped cardboard to fit snugly on top of the ahi cake. Wrap the circle in foil and press onto the cake. Refrigerate with a weight on top for 1 hour.

LEMONGRASS GOAT CHEESE DRESSING

$1/4$	cup lime juice
$1/4$	cup soy sauce
1	Tbs. fish sauce
$1/4$	cup sugar
4	tsp. sambal ulek or 1 tsp. red chile flakes
$1/4$	cup water
5	tsp. lemongrass, minced
$1\frac{1}{2}$	Tbs. ginger, minced
1	Tbs. garlic
4	oz. fresh goat cheese

Combine all ingredients except goat cheese. Strain dressing mixture into a bowl.

Add goat cheese. When incorporated, transfer to a blend-

Bring the Tropics to a Luncheon Table

The beneficent spirits of Hawaiian legend are conjured by the decor for this luncheon
banquet table. The colors and fragrances of the flowers go hand in hand
with tropical fruit to create an informal yet enchanting party. The necessary materials are:

- 3 10" papier-mâché bowls
- 6 bricks floral foam (oasis)
- 7 pincushion proteas
- 5 red alstroemerias
- 4 stems heliconia
- 2 bunches leather fern
- 6 monstera leaves

- 1 bunch ti leaves
- 4 bunches galax leaves
- 5 chamaedorea palm leaves
- 3 bunches bananas
- 3 mangoes and 7 coconuts
- 10 lemons and 10 limes
- sphagnum moss

Of course, various flowers and fruit can be substituted, but an effort to stay with the colorful theme created by the exotica of Hawaii will be duly rewarded.

1. Start by filling the papier-mâché bowls with oasis and water. The bowls can be found at a floral supply store.

2. With the bowls in a row on the banquet table, first cut the heliconias short and put the stems in the bowls at extreme angles. The heliconias can link the bowls and the centerpiece if the inside stems cross one another as they reach from bowl to bowl.

2. Next add the proteas, again after cutting them to form different heights.

3. Add the monstera leaves low to the mâché to cover the oasis, and fill in with the rest of the flowers and greens.

4. Randomly place the fruit on and around the bowls.

5. Finally, cover the bowls with galax leaves and moss. Instead of napkin rings, rest one lime or lemon on the napkin at each place setting.

er and pulse to remove remaining lumps. Do not over-blend or dressing will become too thin. Reserve.

TOMATO-GINGER COULIS

2	Tbs. olive oil
1	tsp. garlic, minced
1/2	tsp. ginger, peeled and sliced
1 3/4	cups tomatoes, seeded and diced
1/2	cup chicken stock
1/4	cup clam juice

Heat olive oil in sauté pan. Add garlic and ginger. Sauté briefly, then add tomatoes and cook 2 more minutes. Add chicken stock and clam juice. Simmer for 45 minutes. Remove from heat and puree in blender. Reserve in a plastic squeeze bottle.

To Serve: Carefully drain off excess juices, unmold ahi cake and cut into 6 wedges. Paint a circle in the center of each plate with 2 tablespoons of Lemongrass Goat Cheese dressing. Place a wedge on the dressing. Dot tomato-ginger coulis around the cakes with the squeeze bottle. Garnish with sprigs of basil and serve.

TROPICAL SEAFOOD SALAD

12	prawns, peeled and deveined
2	1 1/4 lb. live Maine lobsters, cooked and shelled, leaving claws whole
6	Tbs. garlic butter
6	oz. calamari, sliced and cooked
12	oz. ahi tuna, raw, cut into 1/4" cubes
9	slices tako (cooked octopus) cut on diagonal into 1/8" slices
30	asparagus tips, blanched and chilled
1	cup haricot verts, blanched and chilled
3/4	cup avocado, diced
3/4	cup papaya, diced
2 1/4	lbs. total of 3 assorted fresh fish fillets, cut into 2-oz. portions
1/4	cup chives, cut into 1" batons
30	sprigs chervil
1	Tbs. fresh tarragon, chopped
	olive oil for sautéing and grilling

MIXED GREENS AND TARRAGON VINAIGRETTE

6	oz. mixed salad greens
2	Tbs. tarragon vinegar
1/2	cup extra-virgin olive oil
1	Tbs. fresh tarragon, chopped
1	egg
1	Tbs. mustard
	salt and pepper

Combine all ingredients, except greens, for vinaigrette, whisking in oil in steady stream. Reserve.

Season prawns with salt and pepper and sauté in olive oil. Cut up lobster tails, leaving claws whole. Add meat and garlic butter. Transfer to a mixing bowl and add all other ingredients except 2 1/4 pounds of fish pieces, chives, chervil and tarragon. Carefully mix together. Chill and reserve.

Lightly oil and season fish pieces. Grill, keeping varieties separate.

Toss the greens in the vinaigrette and season with salt and pepper.

To Serve: Toss seafood salad with greens and divide in the center of six plates. Place a piece of each fish variety at triangle points around each salad. Garnish with chives and chervil and serve immediately.

LYCHEE GINGER SORBET WITH ISLAND FRUITS

LYCHEE GINGER SORBET

2	Tbs. ginger, peeled and minced
2	cups water
3/4	cup sugar
4	cups lychee nuts, pureed (fresh if possible)
3	cups assorted tropical fruits, peeled and cubed (papaya, pineapple, mango and banana)

Boil ginger, water and sugar together. Remove from heat and strain. Cool. Add lychee nut puree. Refrigerate until cold. Put in freezer for 1 hour. Transfer to ice cream freezer and process.

To Serve: Garnish with fresh tropical fruit.

Fiesta Lunch for Eight

*Featuring Michael Cordua,
Churrascos one and two and Américas
Houston, Texas*

*Corn-Smoked Crab Fingers and Scallops
with Grilled Mushrooms and Warm Huancaina Sauce*

*"We serve a lot of
new food based on a
single premise: It has
to taste delicious."*
—Michael Cordua

Plantains, chayotes, hot peppers, Caribbean cheeses and corn husks, plus a stove-top smoker, are staples of Michael Cordua's cookery, which he showcases in his three Houston restaurants. A self-taught chef from Nicaragua, Cordua is a New World pioneer of Central and South American cuisine.

His chimichurri sauce, an olive oil-based barbecue sauce made with garlic and parsley, is in-

~ M E N U ~

*Fried Plantain Chips
with Chimichurri Sauce*

Robert Mondavi Napa Valley
Fumé Blanc

*Corn-Smoked Crab Fingers and Scallops
with Grilled Mushrooms
and Warm Huancaina Sauce*

*Repocheta Margarita Pan-Roasted
Quesadillas with Achiote-Grilled Shrimp*

Robert Mondavi Napa Valley
Chardonnay

Flan de Queso

Robert Mondavi Moscato d'Oro

an ingredient in cheesecake. Corn husks are an important smoking agent. Layered with water and sherry, they produce crab fingers that taste like "seafood lamb."

"What I am attempting is similar to weaving a basket," says Cordua. "The reeds retain their individual identity but lend their strength to the finished piece."

Cordua, owner of Churrascos one and two and Américas, had an inauspicious start as a chef and restaurateur. As a Texas A&M University student, Cordua had tired of eating daily cafeteria fare. But when he put dried beans into sizzling hot oil, he was left with popcorn and an unrequited, albeit temporary, longing for real fried beans. The next summer, he learned the basics of cooking from his mother and the family's kitchen staff in Nicaragua. He had made a deal he had to keep with his Nicaraguan classmates in Houston. If they would clean, he would cook. He has not cleaned since.

At Américas, Cordua begins with ingredients indigenous to Mexico, North, Central and South America. Using French and American cooking techniques, he invents and re-invents ways of cooking with corn, potatoes, chocolate and coconut. He serves his culinary reincarnations in Américas' surrealistic atmosphere.

Motifs take their cues from Aztec, Incan and Mayan cultures in the restaurant designed by Chicagoan Jordan Mozer. The entryway suggests an Incan temple. Tiled pillars soar, contributing to an effect that is more sculptural than architectural.

Before Américas, there was Churrascos one and two. Before Churrascos one and two, Cordua intended to be a banker. That was before politics in Nicaragua turned his ambitions topsy-turvy. It was his brother, Glenn, a wine aficionado also living in Houston, and an uncle who owned a restaurant in Managua, who inspired Cordua to make his hobby his profession.

In the beginning, there was no way Cordua could have foreseen his future success. His first customers walked out before ordering. But by year's end, Churrascos one was getting national attention. Today, five years later, Cordua owns three restaurants and continues to move forward. He will add a tapas bar to one of the Churrascos to keep pace with his customers' growing in-

spired by tastes from Argentina. His huancaina sauce, a blend of stinging hot aji peppers, cheese and evaporated milk served over boiled potatoes, draws on the traditions of Peruvian cuisine. His open-faced repocheta is created around a South American-styled quesadilla. The origin of his locally famous churrasco, a butterflied tenderloin of beef and namesake for two of his three restaurants, is also South American.

Plantains are "daily bread" for Nicaraguans and standard fare on Cordua's restaurant tables. He serves 2,500 pounds of plantains a week. His stove-top cooker is an indispensable part of every kitchen in his Latin American homeland.

Cordua's signature is a flair for the cooking traditions of Central and South America. Consider corn, the quintessential American foodstuff. Under Cordua's direction, it shares center stage with the plantain. Corn figures into the crust for red snapper and the fettucine dough served with grilled shrimp. It even is

*Repocheta Margarita is served with herbed cream and shrimp
that has been marinated and grilled.*

terest in sampling multiple courses in small portions. He also intends to market his more popular products, including plantain chips and his chimichurri sauce. Under what name? Cordua, what else?

FRIED PLANTAIN CHIPS WITH CHIMICHURRI SAUCE

PLANTAIN CHIPS

4   firm green plantains
    peanut oil for frying

Peel plantains. Using a vegetable peeler, slice plantains lengthwise into long, thin strips. (For best results, peel a few slices starting from one end, then the other.) Heat peanut oil in heavy pan to 325 degrees. The oil should cover the chips as they are frying. Deep-fry slices, one at a time, until golden brown. Remove and drain on several thicknesses of paper towels.

CHIMICHURRI SAUCE

2   bunches curly parsley, finely chopped
6   Tbs. garlic, finely chopped
2   cups extra-virgin olive oil
1   cup white vinegar
    salt and pepper

Combine all ingredients and steep for 2 hours at room temperature.

To Serve: Present plantain chips with chimichurri sauce for dipping.

Cork: The Ideal Bottle Closure

Tradition and performance make cork the ideal wine closure. Its use dates back thousands of years to the Egyptians and Greeks and there is simply no better alternative.

In the late 1600s, it fell to the French monk Dom Perignon to rediscover cork as the best method for sealing wine. In the 1700s, bottles swung into widespread use, and cork became synonymous with bottling fine wines.

Today, after centuries of use, cork remains the best closure for both long-term and short-term storage, according to Michael Mondavi, president of the Robert Mondavi Winery.

Like fine wine, cork is a natural product produced over time. It comes from the bark of a cork

Michael Mondavi

oak tree, Quercus suber, which grows primarily in Portugal.

Nature blessed cork with certain exclusive qualities, making it ideal for sealing bottled wine.

First, cork has great elasticity, unlike synthetic closures. Even when subjected to pressure, cork retains up to 94 percent of its original volume. Consequently, cork is supple enough to be inserted into a bottle neck and to shape itself for a perfect seal.

Second, extreme temperatures have little effect on the cork's elasticity. Cork does not rot. It is virtually impermeable to water and very difficult to burn. That means the quality of wine is preserved and even enhanced during the aging process without concern about the cork spoiling.

Time, however, can dry out cork. To avoid this, bottles are stored horizontally. This allows the wine to keep the cork moist and expanded for a leakproof seal. Red wines, such as Cabernet Sauvignon, benefit particularly from bottle aging. The cork's porosity allows a minute amount of oxygen to enter the bottle, which in turn permits aeration at a desirably slow pace.

Removing the cork is also part of the ceremony whenever wine is enjoyed. Typically, a restaurant will present the cork for inspection. If deterioration is found, it may mean the wine has oxidized and gone bad. Sniffing the wine is the best way to gauge its quality.

An extremely small percentage of corks has natural defects which can impart undesirable aromas, similar to the smell of dirty laundry! Luckily, only one to three percent of all cork-finished wines are affected.

If corkiness is suspected, the wine should be returned to the store for a refund or replacement. In a restaurant, it should be sent back and replaced with another bottle.

Michael Cordua lends a below-the-border twist to quesadillas served with shrimp.

CORN-SMOKED CRAB FINGERS AND SCALLOPS WITH GRILLED MUSHROOMS AND WARM HUANCAINA SAUCE

2	pounds fresh crab fingers or 1 pound shelled Dungeness whole crab legs
8	large sea scallops
6-8	dried corn husks

8	large mushroom caps
1	disposable aluminum roasting pan, 11" x 16" x 3"
1	cooling rack, 8" x 12"

Place corn husks on the bottom of the aluminum roasting pan. Place a 9 x 15-inch rectangle of aluminum foil over husks, leaving a 1-inch border to allow the smoke to escape. Place the cooling rack on top of the foil. Cover with foil, perforating this layer to facilitate smoking.

Arrange scallops and crab fingers evenly on perforated foil. Cover and seal with foil to trap the smoke.

Place roasting pan on top of stove over medium heat. The husks start to burn almost immediately and the smoke flavors and cooks the ingredients in 3 to 5 minutes. Remove from heat and reserve.

Baste mushrooms with olive oil or chimichurri sauce (recipe under Fried Plantain Chips). Broil or grill for two minutes. Season with salt and pepper. Reserve.

HUANCAINA SAUCE

$\frac{1}{2}$	large red bell pepper, coarsely chopped
1	red jalapeño pepper, coarsely chopped
$\frac{1}{4}$	onion, coarsely chopped
$\frac{1}{2}$	Tbs. olive oil
2	Tbs. dry sherry
5	oz. evaporated milk
$\frac{3}{4}$	cup grated Cotija or farmer's cheese (available in Hispanic grocery stores)
1	cup whipping cream

In a sauté pan, heat olive oil and sauté the red bell pepper, jalapeño and onion until softened, about 3 to 5 minutes. Add sherry and continue to cook 1 minute more. Transfer sautéed vegetables to a blender. Add evaporated milk and grated cheese. Puree. Return to sauté pan and add whipping cream. Cook until thickened, 3 to 5 minutes, and strain. Reserve.

To Serve: Coat center of a dinner plate with Huancaina Sauce. Place one smoked scallop inside each mushroom cap and put in center of the plate. Arrange smoked crab fingers in a circle around each stuffed mushroom cap. Serve immediately.

REPOCHETA MARGARITA
PAN-ROASTED QUESADILLAS WITH ACHIOTE-GRILLED SHRIMP

SHRIMP

32	extra-large shrimp, peeled and deveined

ACHIOTE MARINADE

$\frac{1}{2}$	cup extra-virgin olive oil
1	orange, juiced
1	lime, juiced
1	Tbs. fresh cracked pepper
1	Tbs. achiote paste (available in specialty food stores)
1	tsp. ground cumin
1	Tbs. fresh oregano, finely chopped
1	Tbs. garlic, finely minced

In stainless steel bowl, combine all ingredients well and add shrimp. Cover and refrigerate for 2 hours.

QUESADILLAS

8	Roma tomatoes, seeded and chopped
1	cup fresh basil, chopped
16	1-oz. slices Chihuahua or mozzarella cheese
16	flour tortillas

Scatter 2 tablespoons chopped tomato and 1 tablespoon chopped basil in heated, non-stick skillet. Top with one slice cheese and cover with one tortilla. Cook until mixture adheres to tortilla. Flip to warm tortilla. Reserve. Repeat for all 16 tortillas.

To make 8 quesadillas, put two tortillas together like a sandwich. Reserve in warm place.

HERBED CREAM

$\frac{1}{2}$	cup olive oil
6	fresh basil leaves, finely chopped
1	garlic clove, crushed
3	fresh sage leaves, chopped
1	ripe jalapeño pepper, slit on sides
$\frac{3}{4}$	cup sour cream
$\frac{1}{4}$	cup whipping cream

In a stainless steel bowl, combine olive oil, basil, garlic, sage and jalapeño. Refrigerate, covered, for 2 days. When ready to serve, strain out herbs and pepper. Combine seasoned oil, sour cream and whipping cream in a blender and process until completely emulsified. Reserve. (Herbed cream must be made 2 days in advance.)

To Serve: Grill or sauté marinated shrimp. Season. Cut quesadillas into quarters and top each quarter with one grilled shrimp. Serve with herbed cream on the side.

Fiesta Lunch Rejoices in Terra-Cotta

Terra-cotta is this fiesta party's rallying point. The softened, orange-brownish tones of pottery coordinate
with the colors of roses to create a feeling of well-earned laziness and pleasures.
The materials needed for creating the centerpiece made especially for Michael Cordua's
Fiesta Lunch are few and may, in fact, be found in the backyard and garage.

- two 8" terra-cotta bowls
- plastic sheeting or a plastic garbage bag
- 4 bricks of floral foam (oasis)
- 20 garden variety roses, multicolored
- green sphagnum moss

Color is important to this centerpiece of roses in terra-cotta bowls and can be extended effectively if the color of table linens and dishes is integrated. That does not mean matching everything. It means making sure the colors harmonize with one another. Here, colors of salmon, rich blue and green dominate the fiesta dishes in gentle counterpoint to the matching rust-toned napkins and tablecloth, folded for use as a table runner.

1. Before cutting the roses, line each terra-cotta bowl with the plastic. This is to prevent any moisture from the oasis leaking out onto the table. Stuff each bowl with oasis, which has been cut to size and which may include remnants from a recent gift of flowers.

2. Fill the bowls with water and trim any excess plastic that is sticking above the water level.

3. Always cut roses between 5 and 7 leaves down. Cut on the diagonal just above the last leaf. This helps promote growing anew after cutting. To give the centerpiece life beyond the party, snip the ends of the roses off one or two more times, again on the diagonal, to promote feeding.

4. In making the centerpiece, start in the middle of the bowl with the tallest roses first. Add the medium and short roses around the taller flowers. The idea is to build a mass of flowers, creating a sense of bountiful beauty. This centerpiece will be beautiful when viewed from any direction. But if it is to stand against a wall, arrange the tallest flowers in the center toward the back of the oasis and build out from that point.

As a finishing touch, pat moistened moss in place around the stems to cover the oasis and any plastic liner edges still showing.

FLAN DE QUESO

CUSTARD

3	large eggs
2	egg yolks
1	14-oz. can sweetened condensed milk
1¾	cups whole milk
2	Tbs. vanilla extract
5	oz. cream cheese, chopped

CARAMEL

1	cup sugar
2	Tbs. water

In a mixer or blender, combine eggs, yolks, condensed milk, whole milk, vanilla and cream cheese and process for 10 minutes. Reserve.

In a heavy saucepan, melt sugar over low heat to make caramel. Do not stir. When sugar is melted and golden brown, carefully stir in 2 tablespoons water.

Divide the caramel equally among 8 oven-proof flan dishes. Place dishes in large roasting pan and fill with hot water halfway up sides of dishes. Bake until set, uncovered, for 3 hours in a pre-heated 200-degree oven. Remove flans and refrigerate.

To Serve: Unmold the flans into the centers of 8 plates. Drizzle the caramel left in the molds over each flan and serve immediately.

SOUTHERN PICNIC FOR EIGHT

Featuring John Akhile, Azalea
Atlanta, Georgia

Bourbon BBQ Pork Tenderloin, Cheddar Grits and Succotash Strudel,
with Tomato and Balsamic Glazes

*"My interpretation
of ingredients
influences my style.
It's passionate, and
it's heartfelt."*
—*John Akhile*

The new American cuisine is cross-cultural. It's about Asian, African, European, Central American and South American cooking forming the strands of exciting menus with equal emphasis on uniqueness, taste, presentation and good health. It's about choices, and John Akhile, executive chef of Atlanta's Azalea restaurant, stands at the trend's center. Akhile represents the mixing of cuisines that is defining so much of contemporary American cooking.

Akhile, raised in Nigeria and now a U.S. citizen, avoids the term fusion cooking. It sounds like rocket science, he says. Instead, he chooses to describe his work at the high-energy Azalea as "contemporary, new American cuisine."

~ M E N U ~

Vidalia Onion and Country Ham Tart
Three-Tomato Chow Chow

She-Crab Cornbread, Collard Greens
and Smoked Red Pepper Coulis

Chilled Roasted-Vegetable Salad
with Sesame Pecans and Fiery Vinaigrette

Robert Mondavi Napa Valley Chardonnay

Bourbon BBQ Pork Tenderloin
Cheddar Grits and Succotash Strudel
with Tomato and Balsamic Glazes

Robert Mondavi Napa Valley Merlot

Peanut-Caramel Tower with
Peach Ice Cream and Molasses Sauce

Robert Mondavi
Sauvignon Blanc Botrytis

VIDALIA ONION AND COUNTRY HAM TART
THREE-TOMATO CHOW CHOW

TART SHELLS

1½	cups all-purpose flour
½	cup yellow cornmeal
½	tsp. coarse kosher salt
½	tsp. black pepper
1	Tbs. poppy seeds
½	cup unsalted butter, cubed
2	jalapeño peppers, seeded and minced
5	Tbs. ice water

Pre-heat oven to 400 degrees. In a mixing bowl, combine flour, cornmeal, salt, pepper and poppy seeds. Add butter and minced jalapeños. Mix well. Texture should be crumbly. Sprinkle with ice water. Knead until all ingredients are well incorporated and dough is pliable. Form dough into a disk, cover with plastic wrap and allow to rest for 30 minutes, refrigerated.

Roll out dough. Spray 8 4 x 1-inch false-bottom tart pans with spray release. Line pans with pastry. Prick the dough with fork and blind-bake in oven for 15 minutes. Remove from oven and reserve.

ONION AND HAM FILLING

2	Tbs. canola oil
6	cups Vidalia or other sweet onions, diced
1½	cups cured ham, diced
2	Tbs. chopped basil
2	eggs
1	cup whipping cream
	salt and pepper

Heat canola oil in a large sauté pan over high heat. Sauté onions, stirring frequently for 10 minutes. Add ham and continue to cook until onions are uniformly caramelized. Spread mixture on baking pan and refrigerate to cool. Remove from refrigerator and finely chop half of the mixture in a food processor. Do not puree. In a stainless steel bowl, combine the finely chopped ham/onion mixture with the remaining mixture. Add basil, eggs and whipping cream and season with salt and pepper. Return to refrigerator.

Fill each tart shell with mixture. Lower heat to 350 degrees. Bake for 35 minutes or until custard is firm to the touch. Remove from oven and keep warm.

THREE-TOMATO CHOW CHOW

1	Tbs. canola oil
½	cup Vidala or other sweet onion, diced
1	cup red cabbage, diced
1½	Tbs. light brown sugar

Sunflower topiaries invite sunshine to this table
set with plates of BBQ Pork Tenderloins.

2   Tbs. white wine vinegar
1   green tomato, seeded and diced
1   red tomato, seeded and diced
1   yellow tomato, seeded and diced
    salt and pepper

Heat the canola oil in a large sauté pan. Add onions and briefly sweat. Add cabbage and brown sugar and continue to cook until sugar melts. Deglaze with vinegar. Add the tomatoes and simmer for 5 to 8 minutes. Remove from heat and season with salt and pepper. Reserve.

BASIL OIL

2   tsp. plus ¾ cup canola oil
¼   cup onions, diced

2   cloves roasted garlic
2   cups spinach, blanched and squeezed dry, yielding ¼ cup
¼   cup basil leaves, tightly packed
4   Tbs. chicken stock

Sauté onions and garlic in 2 teaspoons canola oil over medium heat. Allow to cool and transfer to a blender. Add spinach, basil and chicken stock. With blender on, add ¾ cup canola oil in a steady stream. Thin with more chicken stock, if necessary. Strain through a fine strainer into a clean container.

To Serve: Spoon a generous amount of chow chow onto centers of 8 warm plates. Place tarts on chow chow. Add another spoonful of chow chow to top of each tart. Drizzle with basil oil and serve immediately.

Making Great Red Wines

All fine wines are born in the vineyard. Truly great wines evolve from truly great fruit. To cultivate fine red wines, care must be given to the very individual characteristics of each grape variety. The most artistic winegrowers gently guide the process, selecting only the finest fruit and allowing naturally expressive and balanced wines to emerge.

Winemakers follow a similar regimen with both red and white wines. It includes harvesting, crushing, fermentation, pressing, maturation, clarification and bottling. But contemporary winemaking emphasizes minimal handling to retain the fruit's full aromas, flavors and colors.

Red wine cultivation requires more time than white wine because of the complexity of the components involved. Red wines commonly are fermented before they are pressed, which is when the juice is separated from the stems and seeds. White wines are pressed immediately and then fermented.

More time is also required for red wine, since to fully develop a red wine of character and depth, extended oak barrel aging is needed.

Red wines are fermented at slightly higher temperatures than white wines (64 to 72 degrees versus 50 degrees) to extract the full color and flavors from the skins and seeds. Fermentation allows the skins to float to the top of the tank, forming a cap that is gently pumped over, mixed or stirred to fully extract the natural pigments and tannins. These are the components that enhance structure and longevity.

The process usually takes five to 10 days to complete. Traditionally, it happens in an open container. Today, jacketed stainless steel tanks are often used.

Sometimes the skins are left with the wine for up to three weeks after fermentation in a process called maceration. This softens wine and adds to its complexity. After the primary fermentation, red wine usually undergoes malo-lactic or secondary fermentation. This softens the wine further. Frequently, a number of red varietals are blended to create a desired style.

Red wine typically is stabilized and filtered before it is bottled. And before filtration, egg whites or gelatin is added to remove astringent substances or proteins that otherwise might cloud the wine or affect the flavor. Sometimes red wine is bottled unfiltered to maximize its richness and character.

It will continue to develop in the bottle after the winery releases it and until it is opened for consumption.

SHE-CRAB CORNBREAD
COLLARD GREENS AND SMOKED RED PEPPER COULIS

SHE-CRAB CORNBREAD

½	Tbs. canola oil
½	cup onions, chopped
1	cup fresh corn (2 small ears)
2	Tbs. roasted garlic, mashed
1	cup yellow or white cornmeal
½	Tbs. baking powder
1	whole egg
½	cup all-purpose flour
½	cup buttermilk
1	Tbs. chopped basil
1	Tbs. soft butter
1	cup whipping cream
1	cup Gulf crabmeat (she-crab with roe) or Dungeness crabmeat
	salt and pepper

Pre-heat oven to 350 degrees. In a sauté pan, heat canola oil. Add onions and corn. Sweat for 2 to 3 minutes. Transfer to a food processor, add roasted garlic and puree. Reserve.

In a mixing bowl, combine cornmeal, baking powder, egg, flour, buttermilk, basil, butter and whipping cream. Add corn, onion and garlic puree and mix thoroughly. Fold in crab-meat. Season with salt and pepper. Spray eight ramekins with spray release and fill with cornbread mixture. Bake for 20 minutes or until a toothpick inserted in the middle comes out clean. Do not over-bake. Remove from oven and keep warm.

COLLARD GREENS

1	cup rendered bacon, coarsely chopped
1	cup onions, julienned
1	cup celery, shaved
1½	cups raw bacon, julienned
1	bunch collard greens, washed and julienned
2	Tbs. minced garlic
1	jalapeño, seeded and julienned
2	Tbs. sage, chopped
1½	cups chicken stock
	salt and pepper

Cornbread, Collard Greens and Red Pepper Coulis

For the rendered bacon, heat a large sauté pan until very hot. Chop bacon and sauté until crispy. Drain on paper towels and reserve. Sauté onions, celery and raw bacon over high heat for a few minutes, stirring constantly. Add collard greens, garlic, jalapeño and sage, and reduce heat to medium. Add chicken stock and rendered bacon. Cook until greens are tender. Season with salt and pepper.

SMOKED RED PEPPER COULIS

1	Tbs. canola oil
¼	cup onions, chopped
2	cups red pepper scraps, smoked*
2	Tbs. roasted garlic
1	cup chicken stock
1	bouquet of basil and cilantro
2	Tbs. unsalted butter
1	Tbs. honey
1	Tbs. dry sherry
	salt and pepper to taste
1	disposable aluminum roasting pan, 11" x 16" x 3"
1	cooling rack, 8" x 12"

wood chips, approximately 1 cup

*To create a stove-top smoker, spread wood chips over bottom of aluminum roasting pan. Cover the chips with a 9 x 15-inch rectangle of aluminum foil, leaving a 1-inch border so smoke can escape. Place the cooling rack on top of the foil.

Arrange red pepper pieces on the rack. To trap the smoke, cover and seal the roasting pan with aluminum foil. Place the roasting pan on top of the stove over medium heat. The chips will start to burn almost immediately. The smoke cooks and flavors the peppers in 10 minutes.

Remove peppers and reserve.

Heat oil in a saucepan. Add onions and sweat briefly. Add peppers, roasted garlic, chicken stock and bouquet of herbs. Bring to a boil and simmer 15 minutes. Remove herbs, transfer sauce to a blender and puree. Strain. Whisk in butter, then honey and sherry. Season with salt and pepper. Reserve and keep warm.

To Serve: Put 2 tablespoons of coulis in the centers of 8 warm plates. Place a spoonful of collard greens also in the center. Unmold cornbread and cut each piece in half, horizontally. Put a cornbread bottom on top of the collard greens. Add another layer of greens. Top with upper cornbread half. To finish, top with spoonful of greens. Drizzle smoked red pepper coulis on the final layer and around the plate. Serve.

CHILLED ROASTED-VEGETABLE SALAD WITH SESAME PECANS AND FIERY VINAIGRETTE

VEGETABLES

1	red bell pepper, seeded and cut into wedges
1	yellow bell pepper, seeded and wedged
1	green bell pepper, seeded and wedged
1	turnip, peeled and wedged
1	zucchini, sliced on bias into ¼" pieces
1	yellow squash, sliced on bias into ¼" pieces
1	carrot, peeled and thinly sliced on bias
2	Tbs. olive oil
24	small basil leaves
24	small cilantro sprigs
16	mint leaves
	salt and pepper

Pre-heat oven to 400 degrees. In a mixing bowl, toss peppers, turnips, zucchini, squash and carrot with olive oil. Season with salt and pepper. Transfer to a baking pan and roast until just tender, approximately 20 minutes. Remove from oven and chill.

GARNISH

1	bunch turnip greens
3	cups canola oil for frying

In a deep frying pan, heat canola oil to 375 degrees. Fry turnip greens until crisp. Remove and drain on paper towels. Reserve.

FIERY VINAIGRETTE

¼	cup	Tabasco sauce
1	Tbs.	garlic, minced
1	Tbs.	maple syrup
½	cup	peanut oil
2	Tbs.	Worcestershire sauce
2	Tbs.	white vinegar
		salt and pepper

In a mixing bowl, whisk all ingredients together until thoroughly blended. Season with salt and pepper. Reserve.

SESAME PECANS

1	cup	pecan halves
½	cup	water
3	Tbs.	sugar
2	Tbs.	sesame oil
2	Tbs.	white sesame seeds
2	Tbs.	black sesame seeds
		salt and pepper

Pre-heat oven to 250 degrees. In a saucepan, combine pecans, water and sugar. Cook slowly, stirring constantly, until all liquid evaporates. Transfer pecans to a bowl and toss with sesame oil and sesame seeds. Spread pecans out on a baking pan and cook in oven until crispy, about 30 minutes. Remove from oven and season with salt and pepper. Reserve.

To Serve: In a mixing bowl, combine vegetables, basil, cilantro, mint and sesame pecans. Dress with vinaigrette and mix thoroughly. Place one serving on each of 8 plates, top with fried greens and serve.

BOURBON BBQ PORK TENDERLOIN CHEDDAR GRITS AND SUCCOTASH STRUDEL WITH TOMATO AND BALSAMIC GLAZES

PORK TENDERLOIN

4	pork tenderloins, 12-16 oz. each, trimmed

sprigs of thyme and oregano for garnish

MARINADE

3	Tbs. balsamic vinegar
1	Tbs. fresh thyme, chopped
1	Tbs. oregano, chopped
2	Tbs. garlic, minced
1/2	cup canola oil
1	Tbs. maple syrup
1/2	cup onion, minced
2	Tbs. chili powder

salt and pepper to taste

In a stainless steel bowl, thoroughly combine all ingredients. Coat pork tenderloins with marinade, cover and refrigerate at least 4 hours.

STRUDEL

16	sheets phyllo pastry dough
1/4	cup unseasoned bread crumbs
1	tsp. chili powder
2	cups cheddar cheese, grated
1	whole egg for egg wash

GRITS

1/2	Tbs. canola oil
1/4	cup onions, finely diced
1/4	cup celery, finely diced
1	cup chicken stock
1/4	cup whipping cream
3/4	cup stone-ground grits
3/4	tsp. turmeric
2	Tbs. roasted garlic, chopped
1	cup cheddar cheese, grated

salt and pepper to taste

For grits, heat oil in a sauté pan. Add onions and celery.

Sauté briefly. Add chicken stock and whipping cream. Bring liquid to a boil and whisk in grits in a steady stream. Reduce heat to a simmer. Add turmeric, roasted garlic and cheese. Let simmer a few more minutes. Grits should be thick and creamy. Season with salt and pepper. Transfer to small baking pan and allow to cool.

SUCCOTASH

1	Tbs. canola oil
1/2	cup onion, diced
2	cups yellow corn
1/4	cup red bell pepper, diced
1/4	cup green bell pepper, diced
1/4	cup yellow bell pepper, diced
1	cup andouille sausage, grilled and diced
1	tsp. fresh oregano, chopped
1/4	cup rich chicken or veal stock
1/2	cup tomatoes, seeded and diced
2	Tbs. roasted garlic, minced
2	cups baby lima beans, cooked

salt and pepper

Heat oil in a large sauté pan. Add onions and corn. Sauté on high heat for 3 minutes, stirring constantly. Add bell peppers, sausage and oregano. Reduce heat and cook 3 or 4 more minutes. Add stock, tomatoes, roasted garlic and lima beans. Continue to cook until vegetables are just tender. Season with salt and pepper. Transfer to a baking pan to cool. Reserve.

To assemble Strudel: Pre-heat oven to 400 degrees. Fill pastry bag, fitted with 1/2-inch open tip, with grits and reserve.

On the work surface, lay out 4 equal stacks of phyllo dough for each strudel. (Each strudel requires 4 sheets.) Mix the bread crumbs and chili powder together. Spray one sheet of dough with pan release and dust immediately with chili bread crumbs. Repeat, using the three additional sheets.

With the short side facing you, spread 1/4 of the succotash evenly over the first 1/3 of the dough. Sprinkle with 1/4 of the grated cheddar cheese. Using 1/4 of the grits, pipe a line down the center and on top of the cheese, the entire width of the strudel. Carefully roll up the strudel. Brush the inside end of the pastry with egg wash and seal. Transfer to a baking sheet sprayed with pan release. Repeat, completing 4 strudels. Bake in oven until golden brown, 12 to 15 minutes.

SAUCES AND GLAZES

BALSAMIC BBQ GLAZE

2	Tbs. canola oil
¼	cup onions, diced and smoked*
¼	cup carrots, diced and smoked*
¼	cup celery, diced and smoked*
3	tomatoes, diced and smoked*
1	cup balsamic vinegar
1¼	cups ketchup
3	Tbs. Worcestershire sauce
3	Tbs. Caribbean jerk marinade (to impart a sweet, hot and tart flavor)
2	oranges, zested
2	lemons, zested
3	Tbs. brown sugar
2	Tbs. chili powder
2	Tbs. bourbon
	bouquet of 1 bay leaf, 1 clove, fresh thyme
2	cups rich chicken or veal stock
	salt and pepper

*For instructions on how to make a stove-top smoker, see She-Crab Cornbread recipe.

Arrange diced onions, celery, carrots and tomatoes evenly on rack resting on wood chips inside a disposable aluminum roasting pan. Cover and seal with aluminum foil. Place the roasting pan on top of stove over medium heat. The smoke cooks and flavors the vegetables in 10 minutes. Remove and reserve.

Heat the canola oil in a saucepan. Add smoked onions, celery, carrots and tomatoes. Sauté for 5 minutes. Deglaze with balsamic vinegar. Add remaining ingredients and simmer for 30 minutes or until sauce coats the back of a wooden spoon.

Strain, pressing the vegetables to extract as much liquid as possible. Divide the sauce into two equal parts. Reduce ½ of the sauce to a thick glaze for basting the pork tenderloins. Reserve, warm.

TOMATO GLAZE

1	Tbs. canola oil
½	cup onion, diced
½	cup celery, diced
6	Roma tomatoes, roasted and peeled
¼	cup roasted garlic
2	cups chicken stock
	bouquet of basil and thyme
1	Tbs. unsalted butter
2	Tbs. bourbon whiskey
	salt and pepper

Heat canola oil in a saucepan. Add onions and celery and sauté gently for 5 minutes. Add tomatoes, garlic, chicken stock and herb bouquet. Bring to a boil, reduce heat and simmer for 45 minutes to 1 hour. Remove herbs from mixture. Transfer to a blender and liquefy. Strain into a saucepan. Whisk in butter and bourbon and season with salt and pepper. Reserve, warm.

FRIED GREEN TOMATO GARNISH

4	green tomatoes
¼	cup buttermilk
¼	cup seasoned cornmeal
¼	cup canola oil
	salt and pepper

Cut tomatoes into ¼-inch slices. Pat dry, dredge in buttermilk and roll in cornmeal. Heat oil in a large sauté pan. Add tomatoes and sear quickly on each side. Remove and drain on paper towels. Season with salt and pepper and reserve.

To Serve: Grill pork tenderloins covered with an inverted stainless bowl, basting often with balsamic glaze. When meat is done, coat the centers of the serving plates with tomato glaze. Cut the strudel into 2-inch-long pieces and place end to end in center of plates. Slice pork and arrange around strudel. Drizzle with reserved, unreduced balsamic glaze and garnish with pan-fried green tomatoes, thyme and oregano. Serve.

PEANUT-CARAMEL TOWER WITH PEACH ICE CREAM AND MOLASSES SAUCE

PEANUT-CARAMEL TOWERS

⅓	cup raw blanched peanuts, finely ground
¼	cup white sesame seeds
3	cups sugar
	pinch of salt

Sunflowers Grace Lazy Gathering

A Southern-styled party conjures up fantasies of linens, languid repose, and fans gently paddling the air above the heads of party-goers. The food will be lingered over, perhaps for hours, as guests relax around a table decorated with bright yellow sunflower topiaries. It is a chance to play to the season, and here is the list of necessary materials:

substitute. Fill the bowl with oasis and then add water. Cut the stems of 10 sunflowers to identical lengths. Tightly gather the flowers' heads together into a round shape and tie raffia around the stems and just below the flowers.

2. To give a finished look, attach two long strips of raf-fia around the bottom of the stems and crisscross moving up the length of the stems to the flower heads. The end result should be a bouquet no more than 3 times as high as the terra-cotta bowl is deep.

3. Firmly insert the stems into the oasis in the center of each bowl and use damp-ened moss to cover up any exposed oasis. Put the topiaries on the table and spread Indian corn and gourds between them.

4. Bunch together 15 stems of wheat and secure with raffia. Make smaller bundles and tie each to a napkin, again using the raffia.

- 3 terra-cotta bowls
- plastic sheeting
- floral foam (oasis)
- raffia
- 30 stems sunflowers
- sphagnum moss
- Indian corn
- yellow gourds
- 120 stems of wheat

1. Line the terra-cotta bowls with sections cut from the plastic sheeting. A heavy-duty garbage liner will

3   cups butter, melted, room temperature
½   Tbs. corn syrup
1   Tbs. milk
1   tsp. bread flour, sifted
2   5¼" lengths of cardboard cut from
     center of paper towel roll, covered with
     aluminum foil

Pre-heat oven to 375 degrees. In a mixer, combine peanuts, sesame seeds, sugar and salt. Add melted butter, corn syrup and milk. Add flour and mix only until incorporated.

Cut 8 rectangles of parchment paper, each 5¾ x 5¼ inches. Scoop 2 tablespoons peanut mixture onto each piece, spreading it over the paper surface but leaving a ¼-inch border. Transfer to a baking sheet and bake for 10 minutes or until golden brown.

Remove from oven and trim excess paper with a knife. Invert paper onto work surface and remove parchment. Roll a cookie around a foil-covered roll, shiny side out. Take care that the cookie overlaps. Press together and allow to cool and harden.

Remove from foil roll. Reserve at room temperature. Repeat 8 times.

PEACH ICE CREAM

1   cup whipping cream
2   cups half-and-half
1   vanilla bean, split and scraped
1½   cups sugar
5   egg yolks
3   cups fresh peaches, peeled and chopped
¼   cup sour cream

In a heavy saucepan, combine whipping cream, half-and-half and vanilla bean. Scald, stirring often. Remove from heat, cover and reserve. In a mixing bowl, combine sugar and egg yolks. Whisk until pale and thickened. Add the scalded cream to the egg/sugar mixture and return to the saucepan. Cook the cus-

tard, stirring constantly over medium heat until it coats the back of a wooden spoon. Remove from heat, strain and chill.

Puree peaches. Transfer puree to a saucepan and cook over low heat until excess water evaporates and puree thickens. Chill. When custard base and peaches are cool, whisk them both into the sour cream. Stir well. Freeze in an ice cream maker. With a pastry bag, pipe ice cream into peanut towers, wrap each in foil and freeze until hard.

MOLASSES SAUCE

5   Tbs. molasses
1   tsp. brandy
1   tsp. vanilla extract
1¼   cups whipping cream

Combine ingredients in a saucepan and heat, mixing thoroughly. Remove from heat, strain, chill and reserve.

PEACH SAUCE

2   cups peaches, peeled and pitted
¾   cup sugar
1   Tbs. brandy
1   cup water

In a large saucepan, combine all ingredients and cook until peaches have broken down completely. Transfer to a blender and puree. Strain and chill.

GARNISH

1   cup whipping cream, whipped to stiff peaks
40   raspberries
8   sprigs of mint

To Serve: Remove peanut towers from freezer and allow to sit at room temperature for 2 minutes. Spoon 2 tablespoons of whipped cream onto center of plates. Place peanut towers on whipped cream and drizzle with molasses and peach sauces. Garnish with raspberries and mint. Serve immediately.

HOT, SIZZLING
PATIO LUNCH FOR FOUR

Featuring Jonathan Eismann, Pacific Time
Miami Beach, Florida

Pacific Time Miso-Rubbed Grilled-Chicken Salad

"America is so big,
and Americans have a
wide-open palate."
— Jonathan Eismann

"I f you want to look like this, eat my food," Jonathan Eismann said as he posed in his shorts for a Miami magazine photographer doing an article on area restaurants. Eismann, chef and owner of Pacific Time, used to be a New York model for boxer shorts. *Ocean Drive Magazine* ran the photograph of Eismann standing on the Pacific Time bar with his quotation below. It worked, boosting sales at Pacific Time, which Eismann opened in 1993.

Both Eismann and his Pacific Time, featuring food with an Asian influence, have hit it off in

~ MENU ~

Pâté Imperial
Poached Shrimp in Rice Paper
with Sizzling Dipping Sauce

Robert Mondavi
Carneros Chardonnay

Pacific Time Miso-Rubbed
Grilled-Chicken Salad

Robert Mondavi Napa Valley
Pinot Noir

Toasted Almond Cake with Warm Bananas
and Sea Coconut Honey

Robert Mondavi
Moscato d'Oro

the slick, hard-edged culture that describes the Miami Beach of the 1990s. In contrast to urbane Miami, Miami Beach is remodeled architectural art deco and home to a young, multicultural, hip and high-fashion crowd. To get a following here, you have to offer something that is exciting, new and consistently good.

Eismann settled on an Asian spin after he conducted the proverbial business study, only to have his own judgment confirmed. There was a surfeit of Latin-influenced cuisine in the area. Plus, there was extensive interest in healthier, lighter, fresher foods, like those typifying the staples of Pacific Rim cookery. "I also happened to be very good at this," he says.

Eismann grew up in New York in a family of graduates from Princeton and Columbia universities and Hunter College. While he had little interest in their intellectual pursuits, he valued their example of a strong work ethic. As it turned out, that work ethic was important in equal measure to both his interests —athletics and cooking.

Both his Viennese grandmother and his mother were valuable teachers. Through his grandmother, he began to understand his own ability for transferring pleasure in the kitchen to the dining experience. From his mother, he had his first brush with the world's cultures through their cuisines. His mother was a corporate chef who kept a multicultural pantry of "objets de cuisine," says Eismann. "One of the best lessons I learned from her was that proper cooking takes a tremendous amount of time."

Eismann had his first restaurant job at age 13. By age 17, he had had four years of people telling him he excelled at the craft he enjoyed. This praise accompanied him throughout his "other career" as well, which lasted long enough for him to realize he disliked the rat race of the New York retail market and to raise the money he needed to open the restaurant in Miami.

On the advice of a friend, he had travelled to Miami in 1987, and liked the area very much. Five years later he was back, money and experience in hand to open Pacific Time. A graduate of the Culinary Institute of America in Hyde Park, New York, Eismann also had spent seven months working at La Table d'Alphonse, a small and highly rated restaurant in Paris.

"I cook with a French head," Eismann likes to say.

Pacific Rim cookery is a vague description for what Eismann sees as his signature work. His pantry is at least as deep as his mother's. His cooking interprets elements of Japanese, Chinese, Indonesian, Mongolian, Korean and Vietnamese dishes.

His focus is on making food healthy, and to do this, he weaves in strands of Buddhist principle and holistic practice. Fresh herbs are critical. Fish is a favorite. Fiber is preferred as a "living food." Vegetables and salads qualify as living foods. Fish and meat do not. Ginger is important as a digestive.

But this emphasis does not mean his portions are small. To the contrary. The best of compliments for this chef is from the guests who "sit down and eat like swine for three hours and then say, 'The great thing about your food is we don't feel stuffed.'"

The average American is overweight, says Eismann. Gradually, more about diet and healthful eating will fall into the food mainstream, particularly as more restaurants emphasize

Shrimp poached in rice paper is served
with Robert Mondavi Carneros Chardonnay.

healthy foods. "If you are overweight, you don't have to go to the gym every day for two hours. All you have to do is eat right."

His favorite post is overseeing dishes as they come out of his kitchen. This is a critical point in the chain of events that takes place during food preparation. At Pacific Time, no heat lights for keeping food warm are allowed. There are no microwaves, no can openers, and no freezers. Deliveries are made each week. Canned goods are not allowed. Fish is delivered from the Florida Keys. Mushrooms come from France and California.

Eismann's emphasis on regional cooking with a healthful twist places him right smack in America's culinary mainstream. His regard for lighter, fresher foods is augmented by his interest in experimentation. "At the same time, I tell myself, if I like liver, it does not mean that everyone likes liver," he says.

PÂTÉ IMPERIAL
POACHED SHRIMP IN RICE PAPER
WITH SIZZLING DIPPING SAUCE

SHRIMP AND POACHING LIQUID

4	large shrimp
1	cup water
1	tsp. sichimi togarashi (Japanese chili powder) or cayenne pepper

The Greening of the California Wine Industry

The most exceptional wine-growing regions world-wide are said to be located between the 34th and 49th latitudes, north and south of the equator. It is within this band that the most ideal climatic conditions for the cultivation of wine grapes occur.

But while a favorable climate is essential, other characteristics are equally important if an area is to grow truly great wines. A region must also possess the soils, the grape varieties and the people who have a passion to excel at consistently producing outstanding wines.

Generally, the cooler and drier the climate, the better. A climate should be cool but with sufficient sunny, warm days to allow the fruit to be brought slowly to full maturity and

Tim Mondavi

optimal sugar-acid balance.

In the 1940s, the University of California at Davis, recognized worldwide as a leader in viticultural and enological curricula, research and experimentation, identified five climatic zones that are suitable for wine grape growing.

UC Davis experts further targeted specific grape varieties that would excel in each zone.

Over the years, the coolest of those five zones— Microclimates I, II and III— have produced the world's truly great wines.

Among the wine regions of the world, Napa Valley is unique in that it possesses not only one of these prized zones, but all three. It also has well-drained soils and people with a passion for cultivating world-class wines.

This diversity of microclimates and soil make-up also means Napa Valley vintners can grow a number of grape varieties, including the classic or noble varieties: Chardonnay and Pinot Noir in the coolest zones, and Cabernet Sauvignon, Merlot, Sauvignon Blanc and

Semillon in the slightly warmer zones. The wines possess extraordinary style while reflecting the distinct regional characteristics found within this special valley.

Beyond the natural elements, vintners and growers throughout California are embracing natural farming techniques in their vineyards, which in turn is leading to more expressive, naturally balanced wines.

This "natural revolution" in California vineyards is being adopted with workers' health, environmental protection, and enhanced grape quality as the goals, says winegrower Tim Mondavi.

As vintners learn more and more about growing their wines naturally, America's tables will benefit with much more exciting, flavorful wines.

1   tsp. lemon juice
½   tsp. salt

In a saucepan, combine water, sichimi togarashi, lemon juice and salt. Bring to a boil. Add shrimp and cook for 2½ minutes. Remove shrimp and slice each laterally into 4 slices. Reserve.

MARINATED CUCUMBERS

1   Tbs. cucumber, very finely diced
2   Tbs. rice wine vinegar
1   tsp. minced ginger
pinch salt
pinch sichimi togarashi or cayenne pepper

In a small bowl, combine diced cucumber, rice wine vinegar, ginger, salt and sichimi togarashi. Reserve.

PÂTÉ IMPERIAL

20   baby red romaine leaves
4   large shrimp, poached (recipe above)
8   mint leaves
½   tsp. marinated cucumber (recipe above)
4   Tbs. miso vinaigrette (recipe under Grilled Chicken Salad)

Hydrate 4 9-inch circular rice papers, one at a time, by dipping them in lukewarm water. Reserve in damp cloth towel. Place 1 softened rice paper on work surface. Put 3 romaine leaves in center of paper, top with 4 slices shrimp, then 2 mint leaves and ½ teaspoon drained, marinated cucumber. Drizzle small line of miso vinaigrette on top of mint. Top with 2 more romaine leaves. Roll like a burrito and reserve.

DIPPING SAUCE

4   Tbs. rice wine vinegar
4   Tbs. water
8   cilantro leaves
1   Tbs. marinated cucumber, drained (recipe above)

In a small bowl, combine rice wine vinegar, water, cilantro leaves and marinated cucumber. Reserve.

To Serve: Divide dipping sauce among 4 small bowls and place on plates. Cut each roll on the diagonal and place one piece on each side of the bowls. Serve immediately.

Poached Shrimp in Rice Paper with Sizzling Dipping Sauce

PACIFIC TIME MISO-RUBBED GRILLED-CHICKEN SALAD

CHICKEN

4   whole, skinless chicken breasts

Rub chicken breasts with marinade (recipe below). Grill or broil, and reserve.

MISO CHICKEN MARINADE

2   Tbs. miso (fermented soybean) paste
1   Tbs. sichimi togarashi or cayenne pepper

Pâté Imperial

2 Tbs. sesame oil
¾ cup peanut oil
2 Tbs. plum wine (optional)
4 Tbs. rice vinegar
2 Tbs. lemon juice
1 tsp. salt

Combine all ingredients in a blender or food processor at high speed for 2 minutes. Consistency should be like mayonnaise.

MISO VINAIGRETTE

4 Tbs. miso (fermented soybean) paste
1 Tbs. minced ginger
¼ tsp. sichimi togarashi or cayenne pepper
1 egg yolk
¾ cup unseasoned rice vinegar
1½ cups peanut oil

In a blender or food processor, mix miso paste, ginger, sichimi togarashi, egg yolk and vinegar. While blending, slowly drizzle in peanut oil. Consistency should be like heavy cream. Refrigerate.

SAKE MIX

1 cup dry sake (available in Asian markets)
1¾ cups lightly packed, light brown sugar

1 Tbs. minced ginger

In a small saucepan, combine sake, brown sugar and ginger. Place over low heat and cook until sugar is dissolved. Do not boil. Cool and reserve.

SALAD

4 Tbs. sake mix (recipe above)
1 cup mung bean sprouts
2 cups coarsely chopped spinach
1⅓ cups coarsely chopped Belgian endive
2 cups extra-thin juliennes of cooked miso-rubbed chicken breasts (recipe above)
6 Tbs. miso vinaigrette (recipe above)
drops of tomato oil (recipe follows)

TOMATO OIL

1 cup Italian tomato paste
⅓ cup minced shallots
½ cup minced celery
3 cups extra-virgin olive oil

In a saucepan, simmer tomato paste, shallots, celery and olive oil for 20 minutes. Remove from heat and let sit for 1 hour. Pass oil through a fine strainer. If cloudy, place back on fire and simmer a few minutes until moisture cooks out. Pass through strainer again, if necessary. Cool.

To Serve: In a small stainless steel bowl, marinate mung bean sprouts in sake mix for five minutes. They should become translucent but not soggy. Drain and save sake mixture in refrigerator for future use.

Combine marinated bean sprouts, spinach, endive and chicken juliennes in medium-sized bowl. Dress with miso vinaigrette and mix well. Divide salad evenly among four plates, drizzle with tomato oil and serve.

TOASTED ALMOND CAKE WITH WARM BANANAS AND SEA COCONUT HONEY

3 large eggs
¾ cup sugar
2 Tbs. vanilla extract

Caribbean Colors Sizzle on Patio

Party guests will sway alongside palm trees — fake ones if the real ones are not available in the backyard — at this party decorated in the colors of the Caribbean. Following are the materials needed to make the palm trees and to decorate a patio umbrella with strings of citrus garlands:

- 8' sprengeri fern garland
- 12 lemons, 7 limes, 20 oranges
- 10 stems bird-of-paradise
- ivy leaves and 20 stems Chamaedorea palm
- wire and sphagnum moss
- 2 5" Styrofoam balls
- 1 6" papier-mâché bowl
- 2 dried yucca stems
- plaster of Paris (quick drying)

1. Using wire, attach the sprengeri fern garland to the top of the patio umbrella pole and spiral it around and down the pole. Cut ½ of the fruit in halves and insert a 6-inch piece of wire through the bottom ends. Then attach the fruit to the garland. Place the remaining whole fruit at the base of the pole.

2. Cut the bird-of-paradise stems to 4 inches in length, insert a strip of wire through the stems and attach them to the garland. Fill the papier-mâché bowl with plaster of Paris that has been mixed with water. Put the yucca stems in the plaster at an angle and hold them until the plaster hardens.

3. Cover the Styrofoam balls with moss, using the wire to hold the moss in place. Firmly press the balls onto the top of the yucca stems and insert Chamaedorea palms into the mossed balls, creating the shape of a palm tree. Cover the plastic base with the remaining moss.

¼   tsp. almond extract
⅓   cup flour
¾   cup almonds, toasted and ground
4   Tbs. butter, melted

Pre-heat oven to 325 degrees. Beat eggs, sugar, vanilla and almond extract together until fully incorporated. Reserve. Mix together flour and almonds. Reserve.

Melt butter and reserve at room temperature. Add butter and flour/almond mixture alternately to the egg/sugar mixture. Line a 9-inch cake pan with a buttered parchment circle, cut to fit. Pour batter in pan and gently tap on table to settle.

Bake until firm and spongy to the touch or when sides begin to pull away from pan, about 20 minutes.

BANANAS WITH HONEY
1⅓   cup bananas, thinly sliced
1   tsp. butter
2   Tbs. brown sugar
2   Tbs. sea coconut or light-colored honey

In a sauté pan, combine ingredients and cook for 1 minute, stirring constantly. Remove from heat and reserve.

GARNISH
    fresh raspberries
    fresh mint leaves

To Serve: Cut 4 slices of almond cake and place one slice on each of 4 plates. Top with banana-honey mixture. Garnish with fresh mint and raspberries and serve immediately.

AFTER-THEATRE SUPPER FOR FOUR

Featuring David Ruggerio, Le Chantilly
New York, New York

Thai Grilled Prawns with Coconut, Lemongrass
and Honshimeji Mushrooms

*"I pride myself on
an unrelenting
commitment to
that all-too-elusive
goal of perfection."*
—David Ruggerio

David Ruggerio turned full-time professional chef after he swore off the first-class shiners he collected fighting in New York's boxing rings. Today, he is heralded for an ability to successfully meld French cooking techniques and daring cosmopolitan menus. His was not an unlikely switch—at least for this first-generation Italian who salts his conversation with the "wids" and "dats" of his hometown, Brooklyn. Boxing amateur or pro—and Ruggerio did both—means center stage, spotlights, sweat, and a passion that is played out before a crowd equally

~ MENU ~

*Cappuccino of Onion with Warm Tart
of Fromage Blanc and Onion*

―――――――

Tuna Tartare Parfait

―――――――

Napa Valley Sparkling Wine

―――――――

*Thai Grilled Prawns with Coconut,
Lemongrass and Honshimeji Mushrooms*

―――――――

Robert Mondavi Napa Valley Chardonnay

―――――――

*Pan-Seared Loin of Rabbit
Stuffed with Arugula,
Sautéed Black-Eyed Peas,
Truffle and Fennel à la Grecque*

―――――――

Robert Mondavi Napa Valley Merlot

―――――――

Crispy Roasted Pear with Licorice Sauce

―――――――

Robert Mondavi Napa Valley
Sauvignon Blanc Botrytis

all-too-elusive goal of perfection.

The challenge that distinguished Ruggerio's career presented itself in 1990. He had worked as chef at La Caravelle, known for its strictly French cuisine, and later at Maxim's, stepchild of the legendary Parisian restaurant by the same name. At La Caravelle, he climbed from saucier to chef, breaking away for a short time to apprentice at the Hotel Négresco in Nice. But it was at Maxim's that he met Camille Dulac, now his business partner.

In less than a year, the pair turned Le Chantilly around, creating a restaurant around Ruggerio's electrifying menus. The blending of Old World refinement and futuristic food dispelled Le Chantilly's earlier reputation as yet another French eatery.

Consider Ruggerio's foie gras. This French menu staple turns into a taste-explosive appetizer under Ruggerio's direction. It is poached with slivers of fresh ginger in a broth made from Gewürztraminer wine and served with green apple shavings produced at tableside. Or consider his ability to raise vegetables from the mundane to the sublime, including the lowly onion. His "cappuccino" of onion, an intense onion broth, only hints at the dimension vegetables add to his menu.

Likewise, Thai food is popular with Ruggerio, particularly because this Pacific Rim cuisine uses few, if any, dairy products. Ruggerio also prefers broths, emulsions and oils over butter and cream sauces.

"While my basic technique draws on the discipline of French cooking, my approach, my mentality is cosmopolitan," he says.

CAPPUCCINO OF ONION WITH
WARM TART OF FROMAGE BLANC AND ONION

FROMAGE BLANC AND ONION TART

2	3" x 6" pieces of finished puff pastry
2	Tbs. vegetable oil
2	large white onions, peeled and thinly sliced
4	Tbs. fromage blanc or ricotta cheese
2	tsp. chopped chives

*A dramatic centerpiece and delicately prepared rabbit
await guests at an after-theatre party.*

capable of cheers and boos. In the ring, competition is neatly defined. And the hands are critical.

The same holds true in the restaurant. "It's demanding, and it's exhilarating. It can make or break you. The competition in the kitchen is between you and the customer," says Ruggerio.

Ruggerio has won praise from America's premier food writers for his work in three of Manhattan's important restaurants, all successful in the burly whirl that is New York City's style. First La Caravelle, then Maxim's, and now Le Chantilly, have served as Ruggerio's ring for showcasing his prowess at turning staid cookery into inspired taste and visual treats.

For the boxer-turned-chef, the draw of the kitchen is the opportunity it holds to work creatively with his hands and to orchestrate the diverse activities that keep a top-flight restaurant going. He prides himself on his unrelenting commitment to that

Pre-heat oven to 350 degrees. Using an inverted cappuccino cup, trace 4 circles onto the puff pastry, cut them out and bake between 2 non-stick sheet pans until crispy and golden brown. Cool.

In a non-reactive saucepan, heat the oil, add onion and cook over moderate heat until lightly browned. Reserve 1 tablespoon of cooked onion for each tart.

The History of Toasts

"Bottoms up!" "Skoal!" and "Zum Wohl!" have prompted people for years to lift both their glasses and their spirits in friendship and greeting. In fact, the tradition of toasting evolves from ancient Greek customs.

At the time of the Greeks, a dinner host gained both the trust and good will of his guests by drinking first from his cup. He was expected to demonstrate that someone had not surreptitiously slipped a little poison into the drink. The expectation gave way to the custom of drinking to one's health and welfare when people dined together.

History has recorded similar customs among the Egyptians and Chinese, both of whom offered wine to guests before meals as a sign of hospitality and friendship.

It was the Romans who refined the custom by improving the wine's flavor. They placed burnt bread in their wine. The char from the toast mellowed the taste.

Thus, wine and toast was literally that, although "toast" was not used as an expression of good will until centuries later in England.

The English, too, used toast in wine, but their own version. During the reign of Queen Elizabeth I, they added spices to the toast before putting it in a goblet. The creation countered the taste of wine that had soured.

In those days, wine frequently spoiled quickly because it was stored in barrels. As the English drank their wine and ate the wine-soaked toast, they bid each other good health repeatedly —until the toast and wine were gone. Thus, the origins of "toasting."

Today, toasting celebrates the wine, the spirit of the occasion and the camaraderie that is associated with people dining together. As a result, people of many cultures continue to develop toasts that are handed down, generation to generation.

CAPPUCCINO OF ONION

Remaining onions from preceding tart recipe
2	cups unsalted chicken stock
1	tsp. fresh thyme, finely chopped
1/2	cup steamed milk
1	tsp. toasted cumin seeds
	salt and white pepper

Add the chicken stock and thyme to the remaining cooked onion. Simmer over medium heat for 15 to 20 minutes, reducing stock by half. Puree in blender and season with salt and white pepper. Reserve.

To Serve: Spread fromage blanc onto each pastry circle. Top each with 1 tablespoon of reserved onion. Sprinkle with chives and warm in oven.

Pour soup into 4 warm cappuccino cups. Top with steamed milk and a sprinkle of toasted cumin seeds. Serve immediately with warm tart.

TUNA TARTARE PARFAIT

TUNA TARTARE

1	lb. fresh tuna, minced by hand very fine
2	Tbs. Dijon mustard
2	Tbs. capers, chopped
2	tsp. Bermuda onion, minced
2	tsp. chives, finely chopped
1	lemon, juiced
	salt and pepper

Combine ingredients and reserve. (Prepare tuna just before assembling so that it does not "cook" in the lemon juice.)

SPICED TOMATO LAYER

2	large vine-ripened tomatoes, peeled, seeded and diced
4	Tbs. olive oil
2	small garlic cloves, minced
1	tsp. coriander seed
1	tsp. fresh cilantro, minced
	salt and pepper

Combine ingredients and reserve.

CUCUMBER LAYER

2   small cucumbers, seeded and diced
2   tsp. champagne vinegar
2   Tbs. olive oil
    salt and pepper
Combine ingredients and reserve.

AVOCADO LAYER

2   small avocados, diced
1   tsp. lemon juice
2   Tbs. olive oil
    salt and pepper
Combine ingredients and reserve.

ROASTED-PEPPER CIRCLES FOR GARNISH

2   red bell peppers
2   yellow bell peppers
1   Tbs. olive oil
4   large basil leaves, crushed
1   clove garlic, crushed

Roast peppers over a stove-top burner until black. Place in a bowl and cover for 15 minutes. Remove skin under cold running water. Remove seeds and tops. Cut into circles, ½-inch in diameter. Toss with olive oil, basil and crushed garlic clove. Reserve.

FENNEL OIL

2   tsp. ground fennel
    Few drops water
6   Tbs. olive oil

In a small bowl, blend fennel with water to form a paste. Mix with olive oil and allow to stand for 2 days.

ROASTED-PEPPER OIL

    Roasted pepper scraps from garnish
10   Tbs. olive oil
    salt and pepper

In a blender, puree pepper scraps with olive oil. Season and reserve.

To Serve: Divide tomato, cucumber and avocado mixtures into 4 equal parts each. Divide tuna into 12 equal parts. Using 4

Loin of Rabbit with Arugula and Fennel

ring molds, 1½ inches high and 2½ inches in diameter, alternate layers of ingredients, starting with the tomato and ending with the tuna tartare. Between each layer, press down gently to bind the ingredients. Take care to use just enough ingredients to cover the previous layer. Repeat the process to build 4 parfaits.

Place the pepper circles, alternating colors, around the top of the parfaits. Plate them before removing the rings. Drizzle plates with flavored oils. Serve immediately.

THAI GRILLED PRAWNS WITH COCONUT, LEMONGRASS AND HONSHIMEJI MUSHROOMS

SEASONED BROTH

4   cups unsalted chicken broth
½   cup onion, finely diced
1   sachet containing 2 kaffir lime leaves and
    ½ stalk lemongrass, chopped
¼   tsp. crushed red pepper flakes
4   Tbs. tomato, peeled, seeded and diced

6   Tbs. green onion or scallion, julienned
4   tsp. fresh coriander, julienned
½   cup honshimeji or other fragrant
      mushrooms
2   tsp. soy sauce
1   tsp. nam pla (Thai fish sauce)
½   cup unsweetened coconut milk

Place chicken stock and onion in a non-reactive pot. Bring to a boil. Add the sachet and simmer gently for 12 minutes. Remove sachet. Add the crushed red pepper, simmer for 3 more minutes. Add the tomato, green onion, coriander, mushrooms, soy sauce, nam pla and coconut milk. Reserve.

THAI GRILLED PRAWNS

8   large prawns (heads on if possible)
4   small coconuts
      salt and white pepper

Lightly season the prawns with salt and pepper. Grill over medium heat until done.

Pre-heat oven to 350 degrees. Cut the tops off the coconuts and reserve milk. Place coconut halves in oven to warm.

To Serve: Ladle seasoned broth into pre-heated coconut shells. Place prawns upright in the coconut and serve immediately.

PAN-SEARED LOIN OF RABBIT
STUFFED WITH ARUGULA,
SAUTÉED BLACK-EYED PEAS,
TRUFFLE AND FENNEL À LA GRECQUE

LOIN OF RABBIT

4   rabbit loins, boned, reserving bones for stock
2   Tbs. butter
6   Tbs. white wine
      chervil sprigs

ARUGULA STUFFING

2   Tbs. butter
4   shallots, finely chopped
4   cups arugula, coarsely chopped
      salt and pepper
Pre-heat oven to 350 degrees. For stuffing, sauté shallots

for 2 minutes over moderate heat. Add arugula and cook for an additional 3 minutes until arugula is wilted. Season with salt and pepper and allow to cool.

Lay the rabbit loins on the work surface with the skin flap facing you, and lightly season with salt and pepper. Divide the arugula evenly among the four loins, roll them up and secure with butcher's twine at 2-inch intervals. In a skillet, heat 2 tablespoons butter and lightly brown the loins. Place the pan in the oven for 7 minutes.

Return pan to the stove. Remove the rabbit, pour off excess grease and deglaze the pan with 6 tablespoons wine.

RABBIT STOCK

      bones from 4 rabbits, cut into 2″ pieces
2   celery stalks, cut into ¼″ dice
1   small onion, peeled and cut into ¼″ dice
1   carrot, peeled and cut into ¼″ dice
4   Roma tomatoes, cut into ¼″ dice
1   bay leaf
1   sprig thyme
2   whole garlic cloves
½   cup white wine
3   cups chicken stock
1   cup water

Pre-heat oven to 375 degrees. Roast bones until dark golden brown. Add vegetables and cook for an additional 5 minutes. Remove from oven. Pour off excess grease and transfer to a 4-quart casserole. Add bay leaf, thyme, garlic and wine. Cook over moderate heat until wine is reduced by ⅔. Add chicken stock and water. Bring to a boil and skim off grease. Reduce heat and simmer for at least 4 hours. Strain and return to the heat. Reduce again by ⅔. Remove from heat and reserve.

SAUCE

6   Tbs. white wine
2   cups reduced rabbit stock (recipe above)
      or veal stock
2   Tbs. butter
3   Tbs. mixed chopped herbs (chives, chervil,
      tarragon)
In a deglazed pan, reduce white wine to 2 tablespoons.

Drama Adds Excitement to Dinner Table

Dinner after the theatre can be simply elegant and elegantly simple — by using a touch of the dramatic to make a statement on the table and sideboard or coffee table. The table for dining should be pre-set and decorated in such a way that the host and hostess continue the suspension of reality that happened earlier onstage. The following materials are necessary:

- floral foam (oasis)
- 8" ceramic vase and 8" vase liner
- 24" ceramic vase and vase liner
- 1½ yards, 54" wide, burgundy-colored fabric
- 1 yard, 36" wide, dusty-rose-colored fabric
- 24" silk cord with tassels
- 15 stems alstroemeria
- 24 dark red roses
- 5 proteas
- 3 Areca palms and 5 Chamaedorea palms

- 10 stems amaranth
- 10 stems dusty rose lily
- 4 votive candle holders and candles

1. Cut the fabric to 2½ times the height of each vase, using the smaller piece of fabric for the smaller vase. Place a vase in the center of each piece of fabric. Pull the fabric up and around the vase, tucking the excess into the top of each vase.

Wrap a cord around each vase neck and tie it in a knot.

Using the oasis, arrange the flowers in the vase liners, and put the liners inside the corresponding vases. The liners can be any object as long as they fit inside the vases. The liner for the taller vase needs to be deep enough to hold the flowers.

The longer the flower stems, the deeper the liner should be.

3. In choosing a vase, an hour-glass shape works best. A cylinder vase does not work well.

Depending on the mood being created, vary the tasseled rope with raffia or ribbon.

Add reduced rabbit stock and continue to cook until sauce coats the back of wooden spoon. Remove from heat. Whisk in butter and chopped herbs. Season with salt and pepper and reserve warm.

FENNEL À LA GRECQUE

4	baby fennel bulbs
24	coriander seeds
2	lemons, juiced
6	Tbs. olive oil
2	cups chicken stock
6	cloves garlic, whole
8	Tbs. white wine
2	sprigs fresh thyme
2	bay leaves

Place the fennel in a saucepan with coriander seeds, lemon juice, olive oil, chicken stock, garlic, white wine, thyme and bay leaves. Bring to a boil and simmer for 45 minutes until tender. Remove from heat and reserve.

BLACK-EYED PEAS

2	Tbs. butter
2	cups black-eyed peas, cooked
2	tsp. shaved black truffles
2	tsp. truffle oil
	salt and pepper

In a skillet, add butter and sauté the black-eyed peas with the truffle. Add truffle oil and season with salt and pepper. Reserve.

To Serve: Place one fennel bulb in the middle of each of 4 plates. Spoon the black-eyed peas around the fennel. Untie the rabbit loins and slice into $1/2$-inch pieces. Place the rabbit around the peas, spoon the sauce on top of the rabbit and garnish with chervil sprigs. Serve.

CRISPY ROASTED PEAR WITH LICORICE SAUCE

POACHED PEARS

4	medium-sized ripe pears, peeled, stem intact
16	leaves phyllo
4	Tbs. clarified butter

POACHING LIQUID

4	cups water
8	Tbs. sugar
2	sprigs fresh thyme

Place the water, sugar and thyme in a saucepan. Poach pears in the liquid over medium heat for 40 minutes or until tender. Drain, core and cool the pears. Reserve.

ALMOND FILLING

2	egg yolks
4	Tbs. sugar
4	Tbs. almond powder
2	Tbs. unsalted butter, softened

In a mixing bowl, combine eggs, sugar and almond powder. Whisk thoroughly. Add butter, piece by piece, and whisk until well incorporated. Spoon almond filling into the bottom of the cored pears.

Pre-heat oven to 400 degrees. Place a sheet of phyllo dough on a dry surface. Brush with clarified butter. Place another sheet on top and repeat process, using a total of 4 sheets, and making 4 stacks. Place filled pear in the center of phyllo sheets and bring the pastry up around it, pressing it together at the top.

LICORICE SAUCE

4	Tbs. sugar
3	egg yolks
1	cup milk
1	Tbs. licorice powder (ground licorice root)

In a stainless steel bowl, whisk sugar and egg yolks together until pale and thickened. In a heavy saucepan, bring milk to a simmer. Slowly whisk the milk into the egg yolk mixture. Stir over low heat until the custard coats the back of a wooden spoon. In a separate bowl, whisk the cooked custard immediately into the licorice powder. Strain, chill and reserve.

To Serve: Brush the pears with clarified butter and bake for 15 minutes until brown and crispy. Serve immediately with licorice sauce.

MEDITERRANEAN DINNER FOR FOUR

Featuring Joel Somerstein, Cafe Pierre
New York, New York

Loin of Lamb with Roasted Eggplant Caviar and Chick Pea Fries

"There's no excess. Food should be stripped down to wonderful flavors and textures."
—Joel Somerstein

There's no substitute for simplicity, says Joel Somerstein, chef at Cafe Pierre, located in the landmark Pierre Hotel across Fifth Avenue from Manhattan's Central Park. It applies both to the task of making up a menu and to the value of accuracy when identifying the right ingredient needed to balance competing flavors. No matter that Somerstein's signature black bass fillet, poached in artichoke broth, is served under trompe l'oeil clouds that play across the ceiling in a room decorated with plush banquettes and gilded mirrors. The basis of this quintessential Mediterranean dish is a straightforward, wine-based broth.

~ MENU ~

Field Green and Herb Salad with
Caramelized Onions and Baked Goat Cheese

Robert Mondavi Napa Valley Fumé Blanc

Loin of Lamb with Roasted-Eggplant Caviar
Chick Pea Fries

Robert Mondavi Napa Valley
Cabernet Sauvignon

Fig and Cinnamon Tart
with Clover Honey Ice Cream

Robert Mondavi Napa Valley
Sauvignon Blanc Botrytis

with Jeremiah Tower at Stars, the San Francisco eatery that helped usher in America's food revolution. There he soaked up everything there was to learn about the emphasis on upscale cooking and food as a restaurant's centerpiece.

The experience, combined with nearly two years on France's Mediterranean coast, did much to shape this young chef, who was destined to carry America's food revolution to one of Manhattan's most formal dining rooms.

Sun-drenched vegetables, the treasures of the sea and indigenous cheeses, oils and pungent spices and herbs describe Mediterranean cookery at its finest. A tomato is not just a tomato along France's south coast. It is simple, yet defined and oh, so very fresh. Potatoes, tossed with olive oil, garlic and herbs, are left all day in the oven's coolest corners to roast slowly until they collapse around their natural juices. Anchovies' natural saltiness invigorate a Caesar salad.

These simple but elegant ingredients are part of Somerstein's style of cooking. He worked in three-star restaurants all over France and learned how the business works. But it took living in the South of France to make the difference. "There, people live outside. They go to the market daily. They come home from work, sit down and enjoy a meal. It's totally unlike New Yorkers, who walk down the street eating their lunches."

His tour of France inspired many of the dishes now on his menu. His fanaticism for onions shines through when he caramelizes the vegetable and pairs it with baked goat cheese to lend a salad an aromatic twist. The onions' natural sweetness combines with the tanginess of goat cheese to make a highly perfumed salad of herbs and greens that, by the way, is also a visual delight.

When he serves lamb, his choice typically is the loin for its leanness. He enjoys pairing it with roasted eggplant caviar, which has nothing to do with fish eggs. The French call it caviar because the eggplant's seeds are part of the dish.

Fruit is plentiful in the South of France, making for delectable desserts any time of the day, any time of the year. "Just because something is simple does not mean it isn't truly great," says Somerstein.

Elegant place settings, wine and fragrant herbs
at table center await guests.

Artichoke hearts are the flavoring in a reduction that produces a sweet, acidic broth which works in counterpoint to the oiliness of the fish.

Clearly, simplicity is the antithesis of what is expected from a New York hotel restaurant. Yet that is precisely the emphasis when it comes to Somerstein's cooking. He learned the basics at the Culinary Institute of America, in Hyde Park, New York. After apprenticing in California, he discovered in the South of France what later became his signature dishes.

But he learned the value of knowing how to taste for the right balance in ingredients while watching his mother at her stove in Woodstock, New York, where he grew up.

His mother, an artist and first-class cook, knew when and where lemon juice makes a difference. She knew how many shots of vinegar are needed to override a dressing's oiliness. She understood the pleasure food offers when it delights both the eye and the palate. But above all, she taught her son to value his ability to decipher what is missing or overpowering in a dish.

After finishing his Hyde Park culinary studies, Somerstein headed for California. It was 1987, and his objective was to work

Pairing Wine and Food

Balance is the key, and personal preference is the only rule when pairing food and wine. Experiment with different combinations — experience can be a pleasant and rewarding teacher. For years, the wine-and-food-savvy have relied on the axioms "red wine with meat" and "white wine with fish". While the approach leads to reliable match-ups, it is passé. Even the very conservative will dare to pair grilled salmon with a Pinot Noir or Merlot and barbecued filet of beef with a full-bodied, oak-aged Chardonnay.

But while the rules have been abandoned, a few guidelines remain to help both novice and expert in making their selections:

• Lighter-bodied, softer wines generally complement lighter foods. Full-bodied, rich, robust wines are at their best with heartier, bold-flavored foods.

• A wine may be selected to complement or contrast with the food. Delicate fruit aromas and flavors of a fine Chablis, Riesling or Chenin Blanc complement the mild flavors and soft texture of a sautéed fillet of Petrale sole, while the crisp, citrus character of a Fumé Blanc or Pinot Grigio is an agreeable contrast with the same dish.

• In selecting a wine, consider dominant spices, herbs, sauces, salsas and accompanying vegetable, potato or rice dishes as much as the main entree ingredient. If the entree is served with a wine-based sauce, it is best to serve the same wine with the meal.

• How food is prepared also should be taken into account. Grilling imparts rich, smoky, wood flavors to meat, fish and vegetables, which are best complemented with fuller-bodied, oak-aged Chardonnays, Cabernet Sauvignons or Merlots.

• Some wine and food pairings have been enjoyed by generations and are too perfect to ignore. They include sautéed foie gras with Sauterne or a Napa Valley Sauvignon Blanc Botrytis, roasted chicken and mushrooms with a Pinot Noir, and grilled lamb chops with Cabernet Sauvignon or a great Bordeaux.

FIELD GREEN AND HERB SALAD WITH CARAMELIZED ONIONS AND BAKED GOAT CHEESE

PÂTE BRISÉE

1½	cups all-purpose flour
¼	lb. butter
2	Tbs. sugar
½	tsp. salt
	pinch cayenne pepper
1	egg
1	Tbs. whipping cream

Pre-heat oven to 350 degrees. In a bowl, combine flour, butter, sugar, salt and cayenne. Add egg, then whipping cream. Mix thoroughly. Roll into a disk, cover and refrigerate for 30 minutes.

Roll dough out ¼-inch thick and press into 4 3-inch tart shells. Prick with fork and partially bake in oven for 12 minutes, until slightly golden. Cool on rack. Reserve.

TART FILLING

3	medium white onions, peeled and thinly sliced
½	Spanish onion, peeled and thinly sliced
6	Tbs. olive oil
4	cloves garlic, chopped
¼	cup butter
1½	tsp. marjoram leaves, finely chopped
10	oz. goat cheese
½	tsp. fresh thyme leaves, finely chopped
½	tsp. fresh chives, finely chopped
	black pepper

Pre-heat oven to 350 degrees. In a heavy saucepan, combine onions, olive oil and garlic and cook over medium heat until mixture is translucent, about 15 minutes. Add butter and 1 teaspoon marjoram. Increase heat, cooking until onions are caramelized. Strain onions to remove excess oil.

In a bowl, mix together goat cheese, ½ teaspoon marjoram, thyme, chives and black pepper. Divide mixture evenly among tart shells. Top with onions and bake until heated through, about 8 minutes.

Goat cheese and onions combine with a field green and herb salad.

FIELD GREEN AND HERB SALAD
2	oz. mesclun
1	tsp. fresh marjoram leaves
1	tsp. fresh thyme leaves
1	tsp. fresh chives, chopped

VINAIGRETTE
4	tsp. shallots, finely chopped

2	Tbs. balsamic vinegar
½	cup extra virgin olive oil
	salt and pepper

In a stainless steel bowl, combine shallots and vinegar. Slowly whisk in olive oil, season with salt and black pepper. Reserve.

To Serve: In a bowl, toss lettuce and herbs with vinaigrette to coat. Season with salt and pepper. Place one goat cheese-onion tart on each of four plates and garnish with salad. Serve.

Guests toast Cafe Pierre's Joel Somerstein.

LOIN OF LAMB WITH ROASTED-EGGPLANT CAVIAR AND CHICK PEA FRIES

LAMB

2 lbs. loin of lamb, trimmed of all fat and sinew

Pre-heat oven to 400 degrees. Season lamb loins with salt and pepper. Roast for approximately 12 to 15 minutes for medium-rare. Remove from oven and let rest.

SAUCE

½ lb. lamb trimmings
4 Tbs. olive oil
1 medium carrot, peeled and chopped
4 Tbs. onions, chopped
1 stalk celery, chopped
3 Roma tomatoes, chopped
2 heads garlic, peeled and coarsely chopped
½ cup white wine
1 qt. chicken stock
1 bunch thyme
1 bay leaf
black peppercorns
salt and pepper

Pre-heat oven to 450 degrees. In a medium-size roasting pan, sauté lamb trimmings until well browned, about 20 minutes.

While trimmings are browning, place olive oil, carrot, onions and and celery in a heavy skillet. Cook over low heat until vegetables begin to brown. Add tomatoes and garlic. Increase heat to high and cook, stirring frequently.

Pour off fat and add browned lamb trimmings to vegetables. Deglaze pan with wine and add to vegetables. Add chicken stock, thyme, bay leaf and peppercorns to the skillet. Bring to a simmer and cook for 1 hour.

Strain out all solids and reduce over high heat to sauce consistency. Season and reserve.

EGGPLANT CAVIAR

1 large eggplant, halved
½ medium red onion, peeled
6 whole garlic cloves
1 medium red bell pepper, charred and peeled
¼ cup Italian parsley, roughly chopped
2 Tbs. extra-virgin olive oil
10 oz. spinach, stemmed
3 Tbs. olive oil
salt and pepper

Pre-heat oven to 300 degrees. Place eggplant, red onion and garlic in a baking pan. Rub with 1 tablespoon olive oil. Season with salt and pepper. Bake for 40 minutes. Remove from oven and cool.

Using a spoon, remove inner pulp from eggplant. Add red pepper to eggplant/onion mixture and pulse to a chunky consistency in a food processor. Transfer to a heavy saucepan. Cook over medium heat, stirring constantly, until all liquid is evaporated, about 10 minutes. Remove from heat. Stir in parsley and 1 tablespoon olive oil. Season and reserve, warm.

In a skillet, sauté spinach in remaining tablespoon of olive oil. Remove from heat and cool. Finely chop spinach, season with salt and pepper and reserve.

CHICK PEA FRIES

1 qt. milk
1 tsp. garlic, minced
1 tsp. parsley, chopped

Fragrance of Herbs Delights the Senses

A Mediterranean dinner calls to mind the fragrance of herbs cooking with vegetables and freshly caught fish. Soft breezes and enchanting vistas complement guests' expectation of a delightful dinner.
This mood also can be achieved in a backyard or dining room by following these tips for re-creating the centerpiece made especially for Joel Somerstein's menu. The herbs, which are a trademark of Mediterranean cooking, are the focal point. Here are the necessary materials:

- wire basket and chicken wire, cut to fit inside the basket
- plastic sheeting
- sphagnum moss
- 2 3″ Styrofoam balls; 2 4″ Styrofoam balls
- 2 grapevine balls
- 1 large and 2 small rosemary topiaries
- assorted small potted herbs
- 4 baskets cherry tomatoes
- wire

Remember, creativity begets pleasure, and entertaining around a Mediterranean theme offers an opportunity to demonstrate the ability each of us has to turn an evening into a special and memorable event.

1. Start by lining the wire basket with chicken wire and filling in the bottom of the basket with the moss. Then line the basket with plastic sheeting, taking care that the moss can be seen from outside the basket.

2. Place the large rosemary topiary in the basket center and fill in the basket with assorted potted herbs, all at various heights.

3. Use the moss to cover the herb containers and to fill in the basket. Place it at the center of the table.

4. Cover the 2 small rosemary topiaries with moss, using wire, and put one topiary on each side of the center basket.

5. Cover the 4 Styrofoam balls, again with moss and using wire. Put a 3-inch and a 4-inch ball on each side of the basket and randomly place the grapevine balls at basket ends.

6. Finally, scatter cherry tomatoes around centerpiece.

1   tsp. mint leaves, chopped
1⅛   cups chick pea flour
1   Tbs. olive oil
     vegetable oil for frying

In a saucepan, bring milk to a boil. Add garlic, parsley and mint. Whisk in chick pea flour in a slow, steady stream over medium heat, stirring constantly to avoid lumping. Cook mixture for 5 minutes. Transfer to an oiled baking pan. With a spatula, smooth out, then chill until solid. Cut into thumb-sized "batonettes" and pan-fry in vegetable oil until golden brown and crispy. Drain on paper towels, season with salt and pepper and keep warm.

To Serve: Cut the lamb into 12 2-inch slices. Place ½ cup of eggplant caviar on each of 4 warm plates. Flatten into a circular shape. Put a heaping tablespoon of sautéed spinach on top and surround with 3 pieces of lamb. Garnish with several chick pea fries. Nap the lamb with the reserved sauce and serve immediately.

FIG AND CINNAMON TART
WITH CLOVER HONEY ICE CREAM

CLOVER HONEY ICE CREAM
2   cups milk
2   cups whipping cream
12   Tbs. clover honey
4   Tbs. sugar
8   egg yolks
     ice water

In a heavy saucepan, bring the milk, whipping cream and honey to a boil. Stir well and remove from heat.

In a stainless steel bowl, whisk together the sugar and egg yolks until pale and thickened. Whisk the hot cream mixture into the yolks, a few tablespoons at a time. Return uncooked custard to the saucepan. Cook carefully over medium heat until it coats the back of a wooden spoon.

Strain and chill in a bowl over ice water. When cold, freeze in an ice cream freezer. Reserve in the freezer.

FIG TART
1   lb. Black Mission figs, stems removed
2   tsp. ground cinnamon
7   Tbs. sugar
1   lb. finished puff pastry dough

Pre-heat oven to 400 degrees. Roll out finished pastry dough and cut into 4 circles, 4 inches across and ⅛-inch thick. Bake the pastry between two baking sheets for 10 minutes or until golden brown. Remove from oven and allow to cool.

In a mixing bowl, mash the figs into a chunky consistency. Dust with ground cinnamon and sugar. Mix well. In a saucepan, warm the mixture through over low heat. Do not cook. Reserve.

To Serve: Place a baked puff pastry disk in the center of each of 4 warm plates. Carefully spoon the warm fig mixture onto each pastry. Top with clover honey ice cream. Serve immediately.

SPORTS PARTY FOR EIGHT

Featuring Todd English of Olives and Figs
Boston, Massachusetts

Grilled Chicken Polenta Sticks

"I want the same layers of flavor, but rolled into food that is of our lifestyle."
—Todd English

Todd English is venturing off in a new direction. His trademark as the owner/chef of Olives restaurant and nearby Figs pizzeria in Boston, Massachusetts, has been lusty flavors and hearty country food. He has emphasized the cookery of France, southern Spain, Greece and especially Italy as he strives to create layers of flavor. But now complexity is giving way to a new emphasis on food that is healthy, light and suitable for customers who, like the chef, love sports and hate stress. While French bistros compete for a place on the American palate, people also want healthy and lighter food without sacrificing flavor or choices.

So what does this new direction mean? "It means I am discarding about a quart of olive oil on a regular basis." Tortellini filled with butternut squash, served with Parmesan cheese, is becoming an Olives staple. Flavored broth is substituted for butter. English's favorite weekend dish is spaghetti with lentil sauce. Grains substitute for meat. Onion rings are dipped in egg whites and bread

~ MENU ~

Grilled-Chicken Polenta Sticks

Lentil and Grain Chili with Raita

Crispy Low-Fat Sesame Onion Rings

*Seared Rare Tuna Crostini
with Arugula and Mustardy Potatoes*

*Savoy Cabbage Stuffed with Figs, Quinoa,
Cabbage, Carrots and Goat Cheese
with a Mint Dipping Sauce*

Roasted Eggplant Mediterraneo

Lobster on the Half Shell

Robert Mondavi Napa Valley Chardonnay and
Robert Mondavi Napa Valley Cabernet Sauvignon

*Lemongrass-Scented Mangoes with
Bananas Coated in Coconut and Chocolate*

Robert Mondavi Moscato d'Oro

how to draw on his Italian ancestry.

His grandparents were in the olive business. Olivia is the name of his wife, who also is his business partner. Oliver is the name of one of his two children. And, of course, Olives is what he calls his restaurant, which opened in 1989 and is now the location of Figs, the pizzeria English opened after Olives outgrew itself. The address of both establishments is Charlestown, a historic section in Boston.

Olives' Grateful Bread is next to Figs. It is equipped with a brick-oven custom-built by a craftsman from Italy's Abruzzi region. And, not surprisingly, a bowl of olives is the daily fare awaiting guests at both of his restaurants.

GRILLED-CHICKEN POLENTA STICKS

CHICKEN AND MARINADE

4		chicken breasts, boneless and skin removed
1/2	cup	basil leaves, finely chopped
2		cloves garlic, finely chopped
1		jalapeño pepper, seeds removed, minced
3	Tbs.	olive oil
1	Tbs.	Dijon mustard
		rosemary sprigs for garnish
		flour for dredging chicken

In a stainless steel bowl, combine basil, garlic, jalapeño, olive oil and mustard. Add chicken breasts and marinate in refrigerator for at least 2 hours. Remove from marinade and grill until cooked through but tender, about 2 to 3 minutes per side. Remove from fire and cool. Slice each breast into four strips lengthwise. Reserve.

BATTER

1	cup	cornmeal
1	cup	all-purpose flour
1 3/4	cups	buttermilk
1/2	tsp.	baking soda
1/2	tsp.	baking powder
1	tsp.	salt

*Checked tablecloths, gerbera daisies and Robert Mondavi wines
complement this sports party menu.*

crumbs flavored with sesame seeds and baked, not fried.

He serves a chunky eggplant dip with tomatoes and low-fat feta cheese. Dessert can be a "Popsicle" of frozen fruit, vanilla and mango sorbet. "As a culture, we are moving toward understanding what is healthy food and what is not," says English.

English still draws on the European influences that shaped his initial cooking style. Especially his Italian ancestry on his mother's side, his travels in Europe, and his work under Jean-Jacques Rachou, owner and chef of La Côte Basque, a classic French restaurant in Manhattan, continue to manifest themselves as English redefines his interests.

From Rachou, this graduate of the Culinary Institute of America in Hyde Park, New York, learned how to marry flavors in a cassoulet and how to make a true velouté sauce. His time in Italy gave him a sense of place and of history and showed him

1	tsp. black pepper
4	egg whites, whipped to stiff peaks

Mix cornmeal, flour and buttermilk in bowl. Add baking soda, baking powder, salt and pepper. Fold in egg whites. Reserve.

Pre-heat oven to 400 degrees. Lightly grease seasoned corn stick molds and place in oven to warm. Dredge chicken strips lightly in flour. Fill each mold halfway with batter, then place one chicken strip in each mold. Fill molds with batter and bake for 15 minutes. Remove from oven and insert a rosemary sprig into the broad end of each mold and return to oven for 10 more minutes or until golden brown. Reserve.

ARTICHOKE-TOMATO SALSA

6	large artichokes

2	lemons, juiced
2	medium tomatoes, seeded and diced
½	small red onion, finely diced
3	Tbs. fresh thyme leaves, finely chopped
2	Tbs. fresh parsley, chopped
1	Tbs. fresh basil, chopped
1	clove garlic, finely chopped
2	limes, juiced
1	tsp. lightly toasted sesame oil

Trim stems from artichokes. Cook artichokes in boiling, salted water with lemon juice until a paring knife can be inserted easily into the bottoms. Remove from water and allow to cool. Remove and reserve several whole leaves.

In a bowl, combine tomatoes, red onion, thyme, parsley,

'90s Wine Varietals and Trends

For most Americans, Chardonnay is the white wine of choice and Cabernet Sauvignon is the preferred red wine. But the world's great wine-growing regions are challenging these habits by piquing the interest of wine lovers who want to discover "new" wines and who want to experiment with wine and food combinations.

Literally thousands of wine grape varieties are cultivated throughout the world. At the same time, only a few are crushed each year to make truly fine table wines. These grapes, which originated in Europe and are classified as vitis vinifera, have proved through centuries of experimentation to consistently produce outstanding varietal wines.

These wines often contain a single grape variety, or they are a blend of two or more varieties. But to be properly labeled a varietal wine, the final blend must contain at least 75 percent of the designated grape variety.

Today's producers of fine table wines are pursuing naturally balanced wines that complement rather than overpower the food they are served with.

This style, which is emerging internationally, is characterized by gentle, more approachable wines that balance complexity and depth with finesse and elegance. They are flavorful wines that express the soils, the climate and the personality of the region of their origin.

While Napa Valley growers will continue to cultivate the "noble" wine varietals—Chardonnay, Sauvignon Blanc, Pinot Noir, Cabernet Sauvignon and Merlot—many also are experimenting with plantings of Italian and Rhône varieties, and their effort is adding interest to American tables. These wines include Viognier, Trebbiano, Malvasia Bianco, Sangiovese, Nebbiolo, Syrah and Mourvedre.

Some of the wines which are expected to grow in popularity include soft, velvety reds—Pinot Noir, Merlot, Barbera and Sangiovese—and crisp, bright whites—Fumé Blanc, Pinot Blanc and Pinot Grigio.

These wines are ready to be enjoyed at the time of their release, and they pair well with a variety of foods.

basil, garlic, lime juice and sesame oil. Remove the artichoke hearts and cut into small dice. Add to tomato mixture. Season with salt and pepper. Refrigerate and reserve.

To Serve: Remove corn sticks from molds and arrange on a platter. Serve with artichoke-tomato salsa. Garnish salsa with reserved whole artichoke leaves.

LENTIL AND GRAIN CHILI WITH RAITA

CHILI

½	cup fresh ginger, peeled and grated
6	cloves garlic, coarsely chopped
2	medium onions, coarsely chopped
3	medium carrots, peeled and diced
3	stalks celery, diced
1	small jalapeño or scotch bonnet pepper, seeded and minced
2	chipotle peppers (smoked jalapeños), seeded and coarsely chopped
1	20-oz. can crushed tomatoes, drained
2	Tbs. chili powder
1	Tbs. cumin
½	tsp. salt
1	tsp. black pepper
1	tsp. fresh oregano, finely minced
½	cup barley
½	cup bulgur wheat
2	cups lentils
1	cup chick peas (pre-cooked)
8	cups reduced-salt chicken stock or water

In a large soup pot, sauté ginger, garlic, onions, carrots, celery and peppers in a small amount of olive oil until onions become soft. Add tomatoes, dried spices, herbs, grains, lentils and chick peas. Add stock, bring to a boil, reduce heat and simmer until lentils and grains are tender, 40 to 45 minutes.

RAITA

1½	cups plain low-fat yogurt
1	red onion, halved and thinly sliced

Stuffed Savoy Cabbage with Mint Dipping Sauce

1	English cucumber, peeled, seeded and grated
4	Tbs. lemon juice
6	large leaves fresh mint, coarsely chopped
2	Tbs. cilantro, coarsely chopped
	salt and pepper

Line a strainer with cheesecloth and rest over a bowl. Spoon yogurt into the cheesecloth and let stand, refrigerated, for several hours. Discard the whey. In a stainless steel or glass bowl, combine all remaining ingredients with strained yogurt. Allow flavors to marry for at least one hour.

To Serve: Raita accompanies lentil and grain chili as garnish.

CRISPY LOW-FAT SESAME ONION RINGS

ONION RINGS

3	medium Vidalia or yellow onions, thinly sliced in rings
2	egg whites, lightly beaten
2	Tbs. sesame seeds
2	cloves garlic, finely minced
1½	tsp. black pepper
½	tsp. salt

Pre-heat oven to 450 degrees. Soak onion rings in egg whites. Drain, then toss in sesame seeds, minced garlic and pepper. Place onion rings on a lightly oiled or non-stick baking sheet and toast until crispy, about 30 minutes.

To Serve: Season with salt.

SEARED RARE TUNA CROSTINI WITH ARUGULA AND MUSTARDY POTATOES

TUNA

1   lb. ahi tuna, #1 sashimi grade

Heat a heavy skillet over high heat. Lightly oil tuna and season with salt and pepper. Place tuna in skillet and sear on both sides, leaving center very rare. Remove tuna and reserve.

MUSTARDY POTATOES

2   baking potatoes, peeled, quartered and boiled until soft
salt and pepper
¼   cup milk
1   Tbs. Dijon mustard

Thoroughly mash potatoes, fold in salt, pepper, milk and mustard. Cover and reserve.

ARUGULA SALAD

8   handfuls arugula or other baby greens
1   medium tomato, seeded and finely diced
1   tsp. capers
1   lemon, juiced
1   Tbs. cilantro, finely minced
8-10   Niçoise olives, pitted and coarsely chopped
1   clove garlic, minced
¼   cup extra-virgin olive oil
salt and pepper
toasted sourdough croutons (3 per person)

In a bowl, combine arugula, tomato, capers, lemon juice, cilantro, olives, garlic and olive oil. Season with salt and pepper and reserve.

To Serve: Place 2 tablespoons of potatoes on each crouton. Layer with arugula salad and top with thin slice of tuna.

SAVOY CABBAGE STUFFED WITH FIGS, QUINOA, CABBAGE, CARROTS AND GOAT CHEESE WITH A MINT DIPPING SAUCE

CABBAGE ROLLS

2   heads Savoy cabbage
2   Tbs. olive oil
2   carrots, peeled and finely diced
6   whole figs, roughly chopped
3   cups quinoa (grain), cooked and cooled
5   oz. goat cheese
½   cup toasted almonds, coarsely chopped
2   Tbs. sesame oil
16   basil leaves, cut into chiffonade
16   mint leaves, coarsely chopped

Remove 16 outer leaves of cabbage. Blanch in boiling, salted water for 30 seconds, remove and immediately transfer to ice water. Reserve. Mince 4 cups of the remaining cabbage and sauté with carrots in olive oil until softened, but still crunchy.

In a small bowl, combine figs, quinoa, goat cheese, almonds, sesame oil, basil and mint with sautéed cabbage and carrots. Remove cabbage leaves from ice water and pat dry. Lay one cabbage leaf flat on the work surface and place 5 tablespoons of cabbage/fig mixture at stem end. Rolling away from yourself, tightly roll 2 turns toward outer edge of leaf, then fold in sides and continue to roll to the end. Repeat, making 15 rolls. The cabbage rolls may be made several hours in advance, wrapped individually in plastic and held in the refrigerator.

MINT DIPPING SAUCE

6   leaves Thai or sweet basil, finely minced
4   Tbs. mint, finely minced
4   Tbs. carrots, peeled and very finely minced
1   Tbs. cilantro, finely minced
1   cup rice wine vinegar, unseasoned

Combine all ingredients in a small bowl.

To Serve: Slice each cabbage roll in half on the diagonal and stand upright on a serving platter. Serve with dipping sauce.

ROASTED EGGPLANT MEDITERRANEO

1   large eggplant
1   Tbs. olive oil
2   cloves garlic, minced
4   oz. feta cheese

All Sports Enthusiasts Are Welcome

Whether the focus is tennis, golf, soccer or ping-pong, a sports party will catch the interest of all those on the invitation list, participants and spectators alike. An outdoor party is a celebration whose success is linked to abundant offerings served from a colorfully decorated buffet table. The idea is to create a setting where guests can eat when and as often as they like. Keep enough mineral water on hand for those who want a frequent thirst quencher. Here are the materials for the table setting:

- green felt
- white tape
- wine bottles minus the labels
- gerbera daisies
- golf balls and tees
- miscellaneous sports equipment

Golf, tennis and baseball are represented on and around this buffet table, but if inclined, bring other sports equipment to the party. A bicycle parked at the side or tennis rackets leaning against the table can be attractive additions.

1. Start by covering the buffet table with green felt. (A green tablecloth also will work.) Use the white tape to outline a baseball diamond on the felt. A checked tablecloth, draped at an angle, adds contrast and excitement. Likewise, cardboard boxes covered in a green and white plaid offer height for displaying a dish or two.

2. Arrange the water-filled wine bottles on the buffet and dining tables. Put gerbera daisies, cut at different heights, in the bottles. Group a few golf balls around the wine bottles and add a handful of golf tees to the arrangement.

1½ tsp. fresh oregano, minced
1½ tsp. fresh mint, minced
1 lemon, juiced
1 medium tomato, seeded and diced
1 tsp. salt
½ tsp. pepper
toasted croutons

Pre-heat oven to 450 degrees. Coat eggplant with olive oil, prick all over with a fork and roast for 35 to 40 minutes. Remove from oven to cool. When cool, cut in half. Scoop out the flesh, coarsely chop it and place it in a mixing bowl. Drain off any excess liquid. Add garlic, crumbled feta cheese, oregano, mint, lemon juice and tomatoes. Season with salt and pepper.

To Serve: Put on plates and serve with toasted croutons.

LOBSTER ON THE HALF SHELL

LOBSTER
4 live, 1 lb. Maine lobsters
3 Tbs. olive oil
1 medium red onion, finely chopped
4 scallions, chopped
1 tsp. ginger, peeled and finely minced
3 large ears fresh corn, kernels shaved off cob
1 Tbs. fresh thyme, finely minced
2 Tbs. fresh basil, minced
1 Tbs. cilantro, minced
⅓ cup balsamic vinegar
1 orange, juiced
cilantro sprigs for garnish
salt and black pepper
ice water

Cook lobsters in boiling, salted water for 8 minutes. Transfer immediately to ice water to stop cooking. Drain. Remove and crack claws, taking out the meat. Cut lobsters in half lengthwise and remove the meat. Discard tomalley, rinse and dry shells. Reserve.

Coarsely chop lobster meat, transfer to a stainless steel bowl and reserve. Warm olive oil in a large skillet. Add onions,

scallions and ginger and sauté for 2 minutes. Toast corn kernels, stirring often, until nicely browned but not burnt. Transfer to a bowl to cool. Stir in herbs, vinegar and orange juice. Season with salt and pepper. Combine corn mixture with lobster meat and spoon mixture back into shells.

To Serve: Arrange on a platter, garnish with cilantro sprigs and serve warm.

LEMONGRASS-SCENTED MANGOES WITH BANANAS COATED IN COCONUT AND CHOCOLATE

MANGOES AND BANANAS
3 mangoes, peeled, pitted and cut into chunks
4 stalks lemongrass, bruised and cut into ½" rounds (available in specialty food stores)
1 lemon, juiced
8-10 large mint leaves, chopped
2 ripe bananas
12 oz. semi-sweet chocolate, melted
1 cup grated unsweetened coconut
sprigs of mint for garnish

Combine mangoes, lemongrass, lemon juice and mint in a stainless steel bowl. Allow to macerate, refrigerated, for 2 hours. Peel bananas and cut into 8 equal pieces. Dip banana pieces in the melted chocolate and roll in the coconut. Transfer to a baking sheet and freeze.

Pick lemongrass out of the macerated mangoes. Reserve ¼ of the mango chunks. In a blender, puree remaining mango mixture with all of the macerating liquid. Add the reserved mango chunks to the puree. Reserve.

HONEY SYRUP
½ cup honey
1½ cups water

Bring honey and water to a boil. Reduce heat and simmer until mixture becomes syrupy. Remove from heat and reserve.

To Serve: Divide the mango mixture among 8 shallow dishes. Place a piece of frozen banana in the center of each plate. Garnish with mint leaves and serve immediately with honey syrup.

Dessert and Sparkling Wine Party for Six

Featuring Gale Gand, Trio
Evanston, Illinois

Triple Chocolate Marquis with Bananas, Praline, Mango Sauce and Espresso Cream

"I come at food first as an artist, then as a cook."
— Gale Gand

If we feast with our eyes before we engage our palates, then presentation influences how we respond to food. This culinary truism applies above all to Gale Gand, the "dessert diva" of Trio restaurant just outside Chicago. Gand's sweet architectural wonders display a creativity in food preparation that sets her apart professionally. In her work, she evinces originality when it comes to spotting the color that is missing in a dessert or a shape that is overpowering a confectionary composition. She knows when a bit of banana or mango sauce will add just the right floral quality to chocolate, or when the grown-up, serious taste of espresso cream is needed to temper otherwise cloying sweetness.

~ M E N U ~

White Nectarine Sorbet Spoons
with Blackberry Sauce

Crispy Fettucine Napoleon
with Raspberry Mint Salad
and Passion Fruit Parfait

Blueberry Bread-and-Butter Pudding
with Apricot Compote

Triple Chocolate Marquis with Bananas,
Praline, Mango Sauce and Espresso Cream

Napa Valley Sparkling Wine

"Food involves all five senses," says Gand. And that includes hearing what guests have to say about her custard or mousse, her chocolate or fruit, which are served in myriad ways on various shapes of granite, marble and glass.

Gand takes unflappable pleasure in being a pastry chef. Whether it involves care in choosing just the right ingredients— all her produce is supplied by a third-generation vendor in Chicago, George Cornille & Sons—or the importance of "accessorizing" tastes, she has a single, unflagging objective: Wow guests with a presentation that attracts both the eye and the palate.

She wants guests to appreciate the texture in her food. Her intention is that they enjoy tastes that complement one another or that collide in creative counterpoint. "This is a great field to work in," she says. "I get to have an intimate experience with people I don't even know. I get to restore them if they are tired. I get to help them celebrate at wonderful times in their lives."

An award-winning pastry chef, Gand is co-owner of Trio with her husband, chef Rick Tramonto, and Henry Adaniya, who is the restaurant's host. Married in 1988, she and Tramonto became "culinary darlings" of media and charity engagements. Their talent for opening restaurants also caught on. Together, they have designed kitchens for 12 restaurant openings.

One of those 12 events took Gand and Tramonto to England. That was in 1990, three years before they decided on the Chicago suburb of Evanston as the site for their own restaurant. In Leicestershire, just outside London, they re-did the Stapleford Park Hotel, garnering in the process a Michelin Guide "Red M" for culinary excellence.

Gand first discovered the pleasure she takes in her profession while working as a part-timer in a restaurant in Cleveland, Ohio. A 19-year-old student at the Cleveland Institute of Art, Gand was an aspiring artist earning her way. When one of the restaurant's cooks failed to show for work, she was asked to help out. She did—and discovered a new career. Today, she still considers herself an artist first and a chef second.

WHITE NECTARINE SORBET SPOONS
WITH BLACKBERRY SAUCE

SORBET

8	white nectarines or $2\frac{1}{2}$ cups
$\frac{1}{4}$	pineapple, peeled and cubed
1	cup sugar
1	cup water

Bring 6 cups of water to a boil in a saucepan. With a paring knife, score the bottoms of the nectarine skins with an "X." Fill a bowl with ice water and reserve. Drop nectarines into boiling water to loosen skins, about 20 seconds. Plunge nectarines into ice water to stop cooking. Peel, coarsely chop and place in a bowl. Add pineapple, puree and strain through a fine mesh strainer. Measure puree and reserve.

To make simple syrup, bring sugar and water to a boil in a saucepan. Cool.

For sorbet, whisk $\frac{1}{2}$ cup simple syrup into fruit puree. Taste for sweetness and freeze according to ice cream-freezer manufacturer's directions.

Baskets of fruit and a plethora of flowers
bring spring to this dessert table.

AMERICA'S RISING STAR CHEF
GALE GAND
TRIO, Evanston
presents
Dessert and Sparkling Wine Party for Six

White nectarine sorbet spoons
with blackberry sauce

Blueberry bread and butter pudding
with apricot compote

Crispy banana Napoleon raspberry mint tea
passed fruit parfait

Triple chocolate mousse with banana,
mango gelée and crispy rice cereal

Sparkling Wine

BLACKBERRY SAUCE

2	cups blackberries
¼	cup apple juice
3	Tbs. simple syrup
	lemon juice, if needed

Place berries and apple juice in a saucepan and bring to a boil. Puree blackberries and strain. Adjust flavor with simple syrup and lemon juice, if necessary. Chill in a plastic squeeze bottle.

GARNISH

3	kiwis, peeled and sliced
6	strawberries, stemmed and sliced

To Serve: Freeze 6 teaspoons. Place 1 scoop of sorbet on each spoon, garnish with slices of kiwi and strawberry and place on plate. Draw a zig-zag of blackberry sauce on the plate next to the spoon. Serve immediately.

BLUEBERRY BREAD-AND-BUTTER PUDDING WITH APRICOT COMPOTE

BREAD AND BUTTER PUDDING

2	cups half-and-half
2	cups heavy cream
pinch salt	
1	vanilla bean, split
6	eggs
1	cup sugar
9	thin slices brioche
2	cups blueberries
2	Tbs. unsalted butter, softened

In a saucepan, bring half-and-half, cream, salt and vanilla bean to a boil. Remove from heat, cover and steep for 5 minutes. In a stainless steel bowl, whisk together eggs and sugar. Slowly

Sparkling Wines and Champagne

"All Champagnes are sparkling wine but not all sparkling wines are Champagne" has a familiar ring to it. But what does it mean?

Technically, Champagne is made from fruit which is grown within the boundaries of France's Champagne region and under strict regulations for grape growing, winemaking and labeling. It is labeled "Champagne" in keeping with European Union regulations. Still, some producers outside Europe's jurisdiction use the word "Champagne"—legally — on labels that provide a generic description of the sparkling wines they make.

To avoid any potential for confusion, a new regulatory regime, created after the 1933 repeal of Prohibition, put in place labeling requirements. A label for "Champagne" not produced in France must include the name of the state or country where the wine is produced.

Still, purists insist that the only true Champagne is made in that small region of France, even though many producers outside that region adhere to the traditional méthode champenoise and rely on French Champagne varieties to create their sparkling wines.

Labels carry information about a wine's style and taste.

Brut characterizes sparkling wines that are dry with no perceptible sweetness. Extra-dry means slightly sweet, though that may seem contradictory. Sec suggests even sweeter wines, and Demi-Sec means very sweet wines.

A variety of grapes is used to make sparkling wines but, generally, the finer sparkling wines use Chardonnay and Pinot Noir grapes, which are the customary grapes grown in the French Champagne district.

Winemakers create the wine's effervescence, clarify it and market it, all in the same bottle. After the cuvée, or the base wine, is selected, sugar and a special

yeast are added to start the secondary fermentation process inside each bottle — this is what creates the bubbles and sparkle.

To reach the desired complexity, the wine is aged for three to five years. Each bottle rests on a rack, neck down, so that the yeast sediment is "riddled," or works its way down to the bottle's neck. The sediment then is frozen inside the neck and removed in a process called disgorgement.

A final dose of wine and sugar (or brandy) is mixed in to adjust for the desired dryness, and the bottle is corked. Only a few more months are required before it is ready to be enjoyed.

add hot cream mixture, whisking constantly. Strain and reserve. Butter and toast brioche slices on both sides. Reserve.

Pour the blueberries into a square baking dish, 8 x 8 x 2 inches. Lay toasted brioche slices on top of berries, overlapping slightly. Pour custard over brioche. Berries and brioche will float. Refrigerate for 30 minutes. Place baking dish into a slightly larger roasting pan. Fill with hot water halfway up the side, creating a bain marie. Bake in pre-heated 325-degree oven until custard is set, about 1 hour. Cool.

GLAZE

¼	cup apricot jam
2	Tbs. water

Bring jam and water to a boil, remove from heat and brush surface of toasted brioche with glaze after baked custard has cooled.

APRICOT COMPOTE

8	large ripe apricots, pitted and sliced
½	vanilla bean, split and scraped
1	strip lemon peel

For years, professional chefs like Gale Gand have enjoyed the opportunities and benefits of convection cooking. Only recently have convection cooking products, like the GE Profile™ 27-inch, built-in convection oven, come into the home. Uniform cooking temperature produces more consistent, dependable and therefore delicious results. Roasts and poultry develop a nice, crispy crust with the juices sealed inside. Baked goods keep their delicate texture while turning golden brown. Many foods, like Gand's Fettucine Napoleon, will cook faster in a convection oven and at a lower temperature. And in baking, all three oven racks can be used simultaneously for even greater time savings.

Crispy Fettucine Napoleon with Raspberry Mint Salad

1	cinnamon stick
¼	cup sugar
1	cup apple juice
	powdered sugar

Place vanilla bean, lemon, cinnamon stick, sugar and apple juice in a sauté pan and bring to a simmer. Add apricots and simmer gently until just cooked, keeping slices intact.

To Serve: Put a large spoonful of bread and butter pudding on each of 6 plates. Put a spoonful of apricots next to pudding. Sprinkle with powdered sugar. Serve immediately.

CRISPY FETTUCINE NAPOLEON WITH RASPBERRY MINT SALAD AND PASSION FRUIT PARFAIT

CRISPY FETTUCINE

1	1-lb. package rolled phyllo pastry #4 thin
½	cup clarified butter, melted
1	Tbs. sugar

Leaving phyllo pastry rolled up, cut 8 ¼-inch slices with a serrated knife, to form strips of dough the width of fettucine. Remove wax paper strips. Gently toss phyllo to loosen and separate. On a sheet pan lined with parchment paper, divide the phyllo strips into 12 equal "nests" about 3 inches in diameter. Using a pastry brush, sprinkle each nest with melted butter, then with sugar. Bake in pre-heated 350-degree oven until lightly browned, about 8 minutes. Remove from oven to cool.

RASPBERRY MINT SALAD

4	cups raspberries
4	mint leaves, finely julienned

Place ½ of the raspberries in a bowl. Puree and strain the remaining berries. Sprinkle finely julienned mint over whole berries. Add raspberry puree. Using a rubber spatula, gently toss berries to coat with puree. Reserve.

PASSION FRUIT

2	egg yolks
4	Tbs. sugar
3	Tbs. milk or 3 Tbs. whipping cream
6	passion fruit, scooped out and drained

In a stainless steel bowl, whisk together yolks and sugar until pale and thickened. Whisk in milk and passion fruit pulp. Place over a pot of simmering water and whisk constantly until light, airy and thickened. Place bowl over ice water and stir occasionally until cool.

Butter an 8-inch x 8-inch x 2-inch baking dish. Line it with plastic wrap and freeze.

Once yolks are cool, fold in whipped cream and passion fruit mixture. Spread parfait mixture evenly in baking dish. Cover with plastic wrap and freeze.

SAUCES

1	cup loosely whipped cream
24	passion fruit, scooped out and pureed to make 12 Tbs.
1½	cups raspberries, pureed and strained
	powdered sugar

To Serve: Cut the parfait into 6 equal squares. Return to the freezer. On each of 6 plates, drizzle sauces in a ring, starting with the whipped cream, followed by the passion fruit puree, then the raspberry puree.

Place one crispy fettucine nest in the center of each plate. Top with a spoonful of raspberry mint salad. Place a square of parfait on top of raspberry salad. Cover the parfait with another crispy fettucine nest. Sprinkle with powdered sugar. Serve immediately.

TRIPLE CHOCOLATE MARQUIS WITH BANANAS, PRALINE, MANGO SAUCE AND ESPRESSO CREAM

CHOCOLATE COLLARS

3	oz. semi-sweet chocolate
3	oz. white chocolate
	cocoa powder
	powdered sugar

Melt semi-sweet chocolate and white chocolate separately in double boilers. Remove from heat and reserve separately.

Cut 6 pieces of aluminum foil, each 7 inches by 4½ inches. Fold each three times to form 7-inch strips that are 3½ inches wide. Each strip will form a high-collared mold for a marquis.

Drizzle a teaspoonful of each chocolate onto a strip, spreading into a thin, even coating over entire surface. Bend strips into circles with chocolate facing inward. Secure into ring-shapes with household tape. Place on a parchment paper-lined sheet pan. Chill.

PRALINE DISKS

2	oz. milk chocolate
2	Tbs. toasted hazelnut, finely chopped

Melt milk chocolate in a double boiler. Stir in hazelnuts. Spread mixture to a thickness of ³⁄₁₆-inch on a piece of parchment paper. Refrigerate until solid.

MOUSSE

5	oz. semi-sweet chocolate
¼	cup unsalted butter
2	large egg yolks, at room temperature
2	large egg whites, at room temperature
1	Tbs. sugar
1	small banana, cubed

In a bowl, melt semi-sweet chocolate with butter in a dou-

A Picnic of Desserts on Grass

Create a feast for the senses by bringing an outdoor dessert party to a table decorated to remind guests of springtime. Whether it is a warm sunny afternoon or 20 degrees below zero and blowing snow outdoors, conversation will turn convivial as guests admire a table bedecked with an abundance of fruit and flowers, all arranged on sod. Yes, sod, the variety that makes for an envied summer lawn or makes a lush golf course green. Here are the ingredients to re-create the centerpiece made especially for Gale Gand's dessert and sparkling wine party:

- 4 rolls sod 18″ x 6′
- 5 old-fashioned fruit baskets, preferably with wood slats (green plastic ones will work too)
- 30 floral water pics for holding single stems
- sphagnum moss
- 3 cartons each, raspberries, blueberries; 5 cartons strawberries; 15 apricots
- 10 stems each, ranunculus, purple iris, red gerbera daisies, scabious in various colors; 5 stems orange belladonna

The spectacular centerpiece keys the colors of the apricots and the berries to the colors in the dessert to be served. And everything, except the fruit of course, can be found at a nursery or

floral supply business. That includes the rolled sod.

1. Cover the table with heavy plastic sheeting to protect it from any moisture that is held in the soil. Unroll the sod, leaving a 2-inch overhang at table's edge.

This lends to the aesthetic, but it also helps prevent dirt from falling into guests' laps. Then, cut an 18-inch round piece of sod and place it at table center, providing height and focus to the flowers and fruit baskets which will spill out in glorious abundance. Stuff a bit of moss or green tissue paper in the bottom of the baskets to help create a feel-

ing of delicious prosperity.

2. Cut the flowers at different heights, making sure that none interfere with guests talking across the table. Cutting each stem on the diagonal helps a flower drink the water inside each floral water pic.

Arrange the flowers, putting the tallest ones at table center and working out from there. Insert each flower into a floral pic, and then push the pic into the sod. Dampen the green moss and cover the top of each pic as well as the edges of the 18-inch round of sod.

Since guests will be viewing the centerpiece from all sides, place the fruit baskets creatively around the table, using a wedge of sod or moss to prop them up in various ways.

ble boiler. Cool slightly. Whisk egg yolks into chocolate mixture. In a clean bowl, whisk egg whites until stiff but not dry. Add sugar and continue whisking until dissolved, about 30 seconds. Fold whites into chocolate mixture. Then fold in banana cubes. Reserve.

ESPRESSO SAUCE

1	cup whipping cream
1	Tbs. light brown sugar
1	Tbs. cold espresso

Lightly whip cream, brown sugar and espresso together until thickened but pourable. Reserve.

MANGO SAUCE

| 1 | ripe mango, peeled and pitted |
| 1/2 | lime, juiced |

Puree mango and blend with lime juice. Strain and reserve.

With a cookie cutter, cut 6 circles from the hardened praline mixture, making each slightly smaller than the foil collars. Place one disk in the bottom of each collar. Fill to the top with the mousse. Refrigerate for at least 2 hours.

To Serve: Gently, but quickly, peel the aluminum strips away from the chocolate collars. Place on plates and sprinkle with cocoa and powdered sugar. Decorate plates with espresso cream and mango sauce. Serve immediately.

INDEX